ISRAEL SINCE 1980

Israel is no longer the country it was at independence in 1948. Over the last quarter century, a radical demographic, economic, and political transformation has been taking place from within. Israelis are beginning to ask some fundamental questions about the country they live in and what it means to be an Israeli. These questions receive different answers, which reflect the changing nature of Israeli society and its fragmentation into different groups. This book, written by five Israeli academics, considers the deep rifts in Israeli society caused by ethnic, cultural, class, and religious divides over the last quarter century. It looks at political and economic changes and how the welfare state has been undermined by the moves to privatization. It questions the role of the military in the light of the wider social and economic changes. Finally, and crucially, it asks whether new political initiatives can offer a realistic alternative to the inadequacies of recent governments. This is an informed and informative account of Israel's recent past and the challenges it faces in the twenty-first century.

GUY BEN-PORAT is Lecturer in the Department of Public Policy and Administration at Ben-Gurion University of the Negev, Beer-Sheva, Israel. His publications include *Global Liberalism, Local Populism: Peace and Conflict in Israel/Palestine and Northern Ireland* (2006).

YAGIL LEVY teaches in the Department of Public Policy and Administration at Ben-Gurion University. He is the author of *From "People's Army" to "Army of the Peripheries"* (2007, in Hebrew) and *Israel's Materialist Militarism* (2007).

SHLOMO MIZRAHI is Senior Lecturer in the Department of Public Policy and Administration at Ben-Gurion University. He is the co-author of *Public Policy between Society and the Court in Israel* (2006).

ARYE NAOR is Associate Professor in the Department of Public Policy at Ben-Gurion University, specializing in the Israeli right, Chair of the Academic Committee at the Jabotinsky Institute in Israel, and a former Secretary to the Cabinet (1977–82). His book *Greater Israel: Theology and Policy* (2001) won the Israeli Political Science Association's Prize for the best Hebrew book in the discipline.

EREZ TZFADIA is Lecturer in the Department of Public Policy at Sapir College, Israel. He is co-author of *Policy and Identity in Development Towns: The Case of North-African Immigrants, 1952–1998* (1999).

THE WORLD
Since 1980

This new series is designed to examine politics, economics, and social change in important countries and regions over the past two and a half decades. No prior background knowledge of a given country is required by readers. The books are written by leading social scientists.

Titles in the series

ISRAEL
Since 1980

Guy Ben-Porat,
Yagil Levy,
Shlomo Mizrahi,
Arye Naor, and
Erez Tzfadia

CAMBRIDGE
UNIVERSITY PRESS

CAMBRIDGE UNIVERSITY PRESS
Cambridge, New York, Melbourne, Madrid, Cape Town, Singapore, São Paulo, Delhi

Cambridge University Press
The Edinburgh Building, Cambridge CB2 8RU, UK

Published in the United States of America by Cambridge University Press, New York

www.cambridge.org
Information on this title: www.cambridge.org/9780521671859

© Cambridge University Press 2008

First published 2008

Printed in the United Kingdom at the University Press, Cambridge

A catalogue record for this publication is available from the British Library

ISBN 978-0-521-85592-1 hardback
ISBN 978-0-521-67185-9 paperback

Contents

Figures

Tables

Abbreviations

DOP	Declaration of Principles
FSU	former Soviet Union
HCJ	High Court of Justice
IDF	Israel Defense Forces
NGO	non-governmental organization
NRP	National Religious Party
OECD	Organization for Economic Cooperation and Development
PLO	Palestine Liberation Organization

Introduction

Guy Ben-Porat

Turbulence seems like the proper word to describe Israel since 1980, and especially the two summers between which this book was written (2005 and 2006). In the summer of 2005, after thirty-eight years of occupation, Israel unilaterally withdrew from the Gaza Strip, demolished the Jewish settlements it had built, and returned to its pre-1967 borders. After months of tension, with various demonstrations and protests, the Israeli army and police moved in to evacuate the settlements, and the subsequent emotional clashes were shown worldwide. Israelis were expecting a quiet summer in 2006, with a new government, elected just four months previously, settling in. However, the kidnapping of an Israeli soldier on the Gaza border on June 25 and the inevitable Israeli retaliation were the prelude to yet more turmoil. Less than a month later, Hezbollah guerrillas on the Lebanese border attacked an Israeli patrol and kidnapped two soldiers. Israel's retaliatory air bombardments and Hezbollah's shelling of Northern Israel escalated into a ground war in Lebanon that ended after a month with a UN-brokered ceasefire. At the time of writing Israel is still painfully researching and debating the causes, management, and consequences of the so-called Second Lebanon War.

Significant changes in the past quarter-century have transformed Israel demographically, spatially, economically, and politically. To a large extent it has since the 1980s evolved into a state and society riddled with existential questions such as "What is Israel?"; "Who is an Israeli?"; and "What does it mean to be an Israeli?" The variety of answers these questions receive reflects the changing nature of Israeli society, its fragmentation into different groups, and its struggle to find definitive solutions to its problems. The turbulent twenty-five years discussed in this book have generated more open-ended questions than answers for Israel's future.

Israel entered the 1980s with two significant developments: an end to almost thirty years of Labor Party domination and the victory of the Likud in the elections of 1977; and a first peace agreement with Egypt (1979), based on withdrawal from territories captured in the war of 1967. Events, however, continued to unfold. A brief chronology of events could include spiraling inflation and a new economic plan (1981–85); a war in Lebanon (1982); a Palestinian uprising in the West Bank and Gaza (1987); massive immigration from the former Soviet Union (1990); a peace process with the Palestinians (1993); the assassination of Prime Minister Rabin (1995); the withdrawal from Lebanon (2000); the collapse of the peace process with the Palestinians (2000); the withdrawal from Gaza (2005); and the Second Lebanon War (2006).

Close to its sixtieth anniversary and with a population of almost seven million, Israel is still a state in the making, whose borders and boundaries remain to be determined amidst growing tensions and crises. These debates pertain not only to Israel's "external" borders vis-à-vis its neighboring states and Palestinians, but also to its "internal" debates over identity, belonging, and citizenship rights. Social scientists studying Israeli society have pointed to the contradictory developments of the past quarter-century. On the one hand, Israeli society and state have integrated globally and the economy has demonstrated significant growth that ranks it among the developed countries of the world. On the other hand, intensifying conflicts within Israel and between Israel and the Palestinians undermine its ability to govern effectively and its international status and, consequently, have held back its global integration. Accordingly, the State of Israel's democratic dispensation has for the last two decades been a source of concern for many Israelis who fear that intensifying social cleavages – national, ethnic, religious, ideological, and socio-economic – undermine social solidarity, overburden the political system, and impede the functioning of Israeli democracy to the dangerous point of "ungovernability."

Israel's tense relations with neighboring states – Syria and Lebanon – and its ongoing conflict with the Palestinians in the occupied territories absorb most of the society's political energies and, politically speaking, constitute the central dividing-line between hawks and doves. Not only is Israel debating its external borders and the related questions of "land for peace," it is also constantly reviewing its internal boundaries and its ability to balance its commitments of a "Jewish" and a "democratic" state. The definition of a "Jewish and democratic state" founded in Israel's declaration of independence underscores, on the one hand, the debates over minorities' rights and, on the other hand, those over church and state relations.

Thus, within Israel an Arab minority is demanding a secure place within the state, contesting its marginal political and economic status and the overarching definition of a "Jewish state." These tensions have resulted in hostile verbal exchanges as well as violent clashes, culminating in 2000 when the police shot dead thirteen demonstrators. The religious–secular struggle is another source of concern, as the previous "status quo" was incompatible with the demographic, economic, and political changes. Officially, religious orthodoxy still holds the monopoly over significant aspects of life (for example, there is no civil marriage in Israel and Jews can be married only by the Orthodox rabbinate) and laws protect the status of the Sabbath. In practice, however, alternative marital arrangements and commercial interests are rapidly secularizing the public sphere and rendering old arrangements irrelevant.

Demographically, Israel has been transformed since the 1990s by a mass immigration from the former Soviet Union, which added more than a million people to its existing population and was one of the factors behind the economic growth of the period. While this immigration has changed the Jewish–Arab balance and supposedly strengthened the Jewish character of the state, it also had a significant secularizing influence. The secular tradition and the fact that many of the immigrants were not Jewish added to the ongoing debate over the Jewish character of the state and further challenged existing norms and institutions. The immigrants' ability to organize politically and to create their own services – media, entertainment, and education – prevented any possibility of quick assimilation or a "melting-pot."

The rapid economic development of the past two decades offers new incentives and opportunities while feeding old tensions and creating new ones. As elsewhere, rapid growth accentuates the difference between society's center and those on the peripheries, who are often left behind. The globalization of Israel is not only of cultural significance, relating to struggles over questions of traditions and identity; it also raises socio-economic questions and blurs the boundaries between public and private. The transformation of Israel towards a market economy and away from a welfare state underscores the debates over property rights, economic rights, and the mutual obligations of citizens and the state. Demands for privatization and tax cuts are matched by calls for the maintenance of the welfare state or requests by politically organized groups for funding of their particular services.

It is of little surprise that these developments amount to a governance crisis. In their seminal book published in 1989, two of Israel's leading scholars described it as an "overburdened polity";[1] this description seems even more relevant today. Surveys in recent years show not only heightened tension between groups that often amount to racism, but also a growing decline in the citizens' trust of government, the parliament, and the bureaucracy. This decline of trust does not translate simply into passivity and withdrawal but often also into independent initiatives that ignore existing laws or into attempts to appeal to different sources of authority, such as the Supreme Court. With government and parliament's inability or unwillingness to take decisions over controversial matters, more and more citizens are appealing to the courts. The Supreme Court's deliberations and decisions have turned it into a significant player, but have also subjected it to severe criticism by those who find it too liberal and, consequently, find its rulings illegitimate. Without a constitution, postponed since 1948 because of internal disagreements, Israel's unofficial arrangements can no longer govern the public sphere. Consequently, the vacuum of authority has led, among other things, to attempts to write a constitution.

These factors are the starting-point of this work, whose purpose is to introduce readers to the political, social, and economic developments in Israel since 1980. It is impossible to capture in one book all the events that have occurred, or the different perceptions and interpretations of these events. What we attempt to do, instead, is to provide readers with an overarching picture, with some "snapshots" of significant events, decisions, and developments. The chapters follow political, social, economic, demographic, and geographic changes, and link them into a coherent story of "Israel since 1980." The different angles and focal points of the chapters capture the various segments of Israeli society – national, ethnic, and religious groups – and their political perceptions and demands.

We begin the book with a description of the structure of Israeli society, its central cleavages, and their impact upon each other and

---

[1]   Dan Horowitz and Moshe Lissak, *Trouble in Utopia: the Overburdened Polity of Israel.* Albany: State University of New York Press, 1989.

state and society at large. The ideological cleavage between so-called hawks and doves is only one of five or so that cut across Israeli society, described in chapter 1. The other dividing-lines include a Jewish–Arab cleavage, a religious–secular cleavage, an ethnic/cultural cleavage, and a class cleavage. All were previously successfully managed by the state by various methods of assimilation, co-optation, and coercion. But now these divisions appear beyond the state's control and threaten its ability to govern effectively. Thus, Israel, like many other states, faces dilemmas that stem from a multinational and/or multicultural reality in which cultural, linguistic, religious, and ethnic minorities struggle for and against distinctive forms of recognition and accommodation and, consequently, create new challenges for the regime.

The cleavages described in the first chapter and the challenges they entail are demographically and geographically grounded. State policies in these domains, in turn, reflect the same challenges of "Jewish and democratic." The second chapter takes issue with demographic concerns and spatial politics that underscore the "Jewish state." First, the practical dimensions of the debate over the external boundaries of the state are explored through the settlement project. Since the 1980s the pace of settlement in the West Bank and Gaza, designed to make Israel's presence permanent, gathered momentum and was established on the ground. Second, the immigration from the former Soviet Union, some 911,000 immigrants who arrived in Israel from late 1989 until the end of 2001, created new needs and demands for land and housing and changed the character of towns. Third, economic growth has brought with it new demands for houses in the suburbs instead of town apartments and contributed to the segregation of space established earlier, enforcing the cleavages. And, fourth, National Outline Plans that sought to balance economic demands with environmental concerns and promote the concentration of the population in four urban centers, with green belts between, were not implemented, owing to intensive activity by various interest groups and the general inability of the political system, described in the following chapter, to provide answers to the challenges presented.

Indeed, the political system, discussed in the third chapter, also reflects the tensions described above and, consequently, displays instability and a crisis of governance. Between 1977 and 2006 Israel has had thirteen coalition governments, with an average of less than three years for each. In other words, the country is living through a permanent crisis of governability that is influenced by the difficulties in resolving the Israeli–Palestinian conflict and in determining the future of the occupied territories and the evolution of the other cleavages described in chapter 1. Attempts to reform the political system, as the chapter shows, have largely failed to curb the fragmentation and bring stability. As mentioned above, with the paralysis of the political system, the judicial system became more significant. But, against the empowerment and growing involvement of the Supreme Court in issues considered "political," a growing opposition within parliament and from various groups has threatened to limit the court's power.

Israel's economic development since 1980, described in the fourth chapter, is also dramatic in its shift from state dominance to a market economy. Between 1974 and 1985 Israel experienced its worst economic period, described by economists as the "lost years." In 1985, when the economic crises came to pose a real threat to the state's fundamental legitimacy and economic viability, an emergency economic stabilization plan was initiated, which led to a dramatic reduction in inflation and in the public sector's budgetary deficit. The significance of the economic plan was not only in the successful reduction of inflation but also in the structural transformation of the Israeli economy, away from its protectionist and state-centered formation to a more neo-liberal type of economy. By the 1990s the Israeli economy was both liberalized, in terms of a shift to market economics, and on course to becoming globalized, integrated in the world economy. The process of "becoming capitalist" was accompanied, as elsewhere, with growing inequality and severe social problems that added to the tensions described in the first chapter.

The military, a central institution of Israeli society, is also influenced by the social, political, and economic developments discussed in the previous chapters. Israelis have long viewed the Israel Defense Forces (IDF) as more than simply the military; in popular mythology, the IDF is "the people's army," a crucial institution for both the defense of the state and the self-image of the nation. But, as chapter 5 explains, the army not only met with a succession of crises after the 1973 war that diluted its resources and reduced its political support, it also became entangled in the political debate and influenced by the evolving cleavages. The war in Lebanon in 1982 shattered the consensus over the military's role and, for the first time in Israel's history, there were protests against the war and even refusals by reservists to take part in it. This has been exacerbated since the Intifada that began in December

1987, when the military presence of Israel in the occupied territories became a major political debate.

Other important developments have been the penetration of cultural and economic globalization into Israeli society, the structural changes in the economy in the spirit of the neoliberal doctrine, and the development of a consumerist society. These changes not only led to a cutback in military spending but also made the military less attractive for the elites who had previously enjoyed the status military service afforded. This "motivation crisis" has made military service more dependent upon concrete material benefits and led to a bargaining process between the military and those who share the burden. Also, the military remained attractive for marginal groups that perceived it as a significant sphere in which to construct new opportunities for social mobility and legitimately attain various civil rights. Its gradual abandonment by social elites, therefore, made the army more representative of the peripheries but possibly more distant from the elites and from the global-liberal civil agenda.

The inability of the political institutions to provide answers to the growing problems has led to new modes of political action. The governance crisis described in chapter 3 underscores the developments of interest groups and an "alternative politics" that bypasses the official institutions and, consequently, renders them ineffective. Chapter 6 engages with Israeli political culture and its evolvement since 1980 in relation to the processes and events described in the previous chapters. During the 1950s and 1960s, Israel's political, administrative, and economic systems were highly centralized; this centralism prevented the development of alternative power centers such as interest groups and significantly slowed the development of a civil society based on liberal values. While political participation through voting during these decades was very intense, other forms of political participation hardly existed. A significant change in the development of Israeli political culture came in 1967 with the Six Day War. It gave rise to nationalistic and religious feelings that were translated into the attempts to establish illegal settlements in the West Bank that would de facto annex the territories occupied in the war. These events expressed the beginning of alternative politics in Israeli society, which had been suspended for two decades, and signaled the governance crisis that unfolded from the 1980s onward. The inability of the government to produce efficient and stable public policy triggered the evolution of alternative politics. As the public gradually gave up legal influence channels, semi–legal and illegal private activities to provide public services spread in many areas of life. The 1980s were characterized by a significant growth of "gray-market economy," "gray-market medicine," "gray-market education," and pirate cable networks.

The purpose of this book is to provide readers with a comprehensive overview of the Israeli state and society since 1980 and the interrelated political, social, economic, and geographical changes. The six chapters, written by five different authors, provide a multi-perspective look at Israeli society, and at times overlap on central issues and developments to capture those perspectives. No attempt was made to establish agreement between authors who, naturally, differ both in their methodological approach and in their political views of Israeli society, so each chapter reflects only the opinions of its author. But, in spite of the differences, the authors do share a concern for state, society, and the democratic regime. These combined apprehensions, we hope, provide a convincing account of Israel since 1980 and the challenges that lie ahead. We will return to those themes in the concluding chapter.

1

Israeli Society: Diversity, Tensions, and Governance

Guy Ben-Porat

In their seminal book published in 1989, *Trouble in Utopia*, Dan Horowitz and Moshe Lissak, two of Israel's leading scholars, described Israel as an "overburdened polity." According to them social conflicts and the frustrations of marginal groups have increased to a point where Israeli democracy is in critical danger of "ungovernability," making it difficult for the system to mobilize material resources and collective normative commitments. While scholars of the Israeli state and society dispute the reasons for societal breakup, as well as its consequences and remedies, there is an overall consensus that relations between national, ethnic, religious, ideological, and cultural groups have become overtly politicized. Israeli society since 1980 has come to accept not only its plurality but also the fact that the existing formal and informal institutions can no longer contain the tensions between groups, but has yet to find agreement on new institutions. The different perceptions of common good and demands for equality and for recognition burden state and society with significant challenges. The contemporary study of Israel, therefore, must first and foremost account for the significant societal changes and their implications for politics and governance.

Israeli society is divided across national, religious, ideological, and ethnic lines; these divisions display not only internal dynamism but also a dynamic relation between them as they constantly affect each other. As a national movement, Zionism has sought to unite all Jews under the umbrella of nation- and state-building projects. The Labor Party (formerly Mapai) became the leading force in the Zionist movement and in early statehood. It combined a socialist rhetoric, a collectivist ethos, a secular interpretation of Zionism, and a largely pragmatic attitude toward settlement and foreign policy. The disputes within the Zionist movement, between secular and religious and between socialists/collectivists and supporters of a free market economy, were largely secondary to the nation- and state-building project, and the dominant Labor Party was largely able to control the disputes. Thus, while ideological differences were significant, the vast majority of parties chose to remain part of the political system, even in the pre-statehood period when opportunities to prevent their withdrawal were limited.

The early period of statehood remained dominated by the collectivist ethos that overshadowed the existing and evolving cleavages. Israel is a country that places high demands on its citizens, most notably a mandatory military service of three years for men and two for women. The demands and privileges, however, are unequally distributed and are part of Israel's stratified citizenship. The larger burden of army service was held by Jewish men and, consequently, accorded them a dominant status in a society that judged citizenship according to their contribution to the common good. The stratification, however, was not only between Jews and non-Jews (some non-Jews, such as the Druze, serve in the military) and men and women, but also among Jewish men. In the early years of statehood the army was dominated by veteran Ashkenazi and secular groups, and it was the entry of new groups – religious, Mizrachim, and immigrants from the FSU – as well as demands for gender equality and the penetration of the privatization ethos that marked the beginning of changes in Israeli society.

The divisions within Israeli society became apparent from the early 1970s. The waning of the Labor Party's dominance in the wake of the Yom Kippur War (1973) and the growing discontent of groups hitherto marginalized in Israeli society undermined the status quo. The change was reflected first and foremost in voting patterns: in the 1977 elections the Labor Party was ousted after twenty-nine years in power. The debate over the future of the territories occupied in the 1967 war (the West Bank, Gaza and the Golan Heights, and the Sinai Peninsula) unfolded into a bitter divide that not only cut across Israeli society but also posed a challenge to the legitimacy of the democratic regime. The question of the territories (the "land versus peace" debate) continues to occupy Israeli politics and has been the central issue of most elections and political debates in the past quarter-century. However, this ideological split between so-called hawks and doves is only one of five or so cleavages that cut across Israeli society. The other dividing-lines include Jewish–Arab; religious–secular; ethnic/cultural; and class cleavages. All were previously managed by the state by various methods of assimilation, co-optation, and coercion. However, they now appear beyond the state's control and threaten its ability to govern effectively. Thus, Israel, like many other states, faces dilemmas that stem from a multinational and/or multicultural reality in which cultural, linguistic, religious, and ethnic minorities struggle for and against distinctive forms of recognition and accommodation and, consequently, create new challenges for the democratic regime.

The External Dimension: Conflict, Peace, and Conflict

The war of 1948 transformed the dimensions of the conflict from an intercommunal to an interstate conflict between an independent Jewish state (with a sizeable Palestinian minority) and its neighbors. The conflict with the Palestinians was perceived as part of the wider Arab–Israeli conflict, and not necessarily the most important part. But, after the war of 1967 and the occupation of new territories, the Israeli–Palestinian conflict regained its centrality. The occupation of the West Bank and Gaza added a Palestinian population greater than that within Israel, about 750,000 in the West Bank and 400,000 in Gaza. Despite the declaration of the Israeli government after the war that Israel had no intention of expanding its territorial boundaries, the temporary occupation was gradually entrenched. The Likud Party, which won the 1977 elections, embarked on a wide-ranging initiative to settle the territories and make them de facto a part of Israel. This, as will be elaborated below, became the central issue of Israeli politics, separating doves and hawks over the question of "land for peace." While dovish parties on the "left" argued that Israel should return territories occupied in the 1967 war in exchange for peace agreements, the hawkish parties on the "right" combined religious, national, and security arguments for keeping the territories.

It was the hawkish Likud, however, that in 1979 signed a peace treaty with Egypt. The treaty, following a dramatic visit to Israel by President Sadat of Egypt, was based on a withdrawal by Israel from the Sinai Peninsula, occupied in 1967, including Israeli settlements, whose residents were relocated to Israel. The exchange of territories for peace was in many respects a precedent and involved debate and struggles between left and right, but its implication for the Israeli–Palestinian conflict were limited. The Egyptian–Israeli conflict was a territorial and strategic dispute much more than an ideological struggle. Israel attributed strategic value to the Sinai as a buffer zone, for which a peace treaty was an acceptable substitute. In a wider, regional, perspective the treaty with Egypt, on the one hand, and the declining commitment of other Arab regimes to support the Palestinian cause, on the other, the conflict, which had been a region-wide, inter-state conflict, has shrunk to its original core, namely Israeli–Palestinian intercommunal strife.

The Lebanon War

Despite the breakthrough of the peace process with Egypt there was no sign of similar developments with the Palestinians. The Camp David framework was vague and characterized by broad guidelines with regard to the West Bank and Gaza, open to different interpretations. The Israeli government was willing to grant only limited autonomy to the Palestinians, neither sovereignty nor self-determination. It set out almost immediately to increase substantially the number of settlers and settlements in the West Bank and elsewhere, taking control of large tracts of land for that purpose (see chapter 5). The government also attempted, by a policy of "stick and carrot," to make Palestinians realize that Israel's stay was permanent. This policy included the detention of "subversive" elements and various benefits awarded to those who cooperated with the military occupation.

The first large and direct clash between Israel and the Palestinians since 1967 happened not in the occupied territories but rather with Israel's invasion of Lebanon in 1982. The Palestine Liberation Organization (PLO) had established a strong base in Lebanon in the large Palestinian refugee camps amidst a civil war that allowed it to operate with little interference. From Southern Lebanon the PLO carried out mortar attacks against the Galilee region of Israel, and Israel retaliated with attacks on its bases. In 1981 the United States brokered a ceasefire between Israel and the PLO, but in 1982, an attempt by a Palestinian organization to assassinate Israel's ambassador to Britain served as a catalyst for Israel to invade Lebanon. What was intended as a short-term operation with a precise military objective against PLO bases in Southern Lebanon turned into a long and costly war, in which the Israeli army occupied part of the Lebanese capital, Beirut, and also fought against the Syrian army. The hidden agenda of the war, which later became explicit, was to crush the PLO in Lebanon in order to establish "a new political order" in Lebanon that would restore Christian domination and impose the withdrawal of the Syrian troops from Lebanon. Practically speaking, Israel was successful only in forcing the PLO headquarters out of Lebanon following the sustained siege of Beirut. However, this move helped Yasser Arafat, the leader of the PLO, to legitimize its political status in the Arab world and to embark on the political road that would lead to Oslo.

The war had important implications for Israel's political divide. Until that war a large majority had believed that for Israel war was not an instrument of policy but a necessity forced upon it by outside factors. This position of "no choice" carried a moral-normative argument that Israel fights "just wars," wars not willed by it but provoked by its opponents. The war in Lebanon enjoyed wide support in its early stages but became controversial as it lengthened and its costs grew higher. There was a fierce public debate regarding its necessity and, therefore, its justness, that deeply divided Israeli society. Despite the government's claim that this war was imposed upon Israel, the opposition argued that because Israel was under no existential threat, all options had to be exhausted before war. For the first time Israelis in large numbers protested against a war – some even advocated refusal to serve in Lebanon. The war ended with the IDF holding permanent positions in Lebanon, attempting to build a friendly Lebanese militia in the south, and fighting local resistance that soon came to be known as Hezbollah. In 1985 the army unilaterally withdrew from Lebanon but established a security zone in the south dominated by the South Lebanon Army while preserving the IDF's presence on Lebanese soil along the border. It was only in 2000, after eighteen years in Lebanon and under internal pressures from citizens' groups in Israel that protested the human cost of the guerrilla war, that the Israeli army completely – and again unilaterally – withdrew from Lebanon.

The Intifada

The Palestinian uprising against Israel's military rule (the Intifada) that began in 1987 shattered another embedded belief among Israelis – that the occupation of the territories had relatively low economic, political, and moral costs. The Intifada began as spontaneous civil dis-obedience when Palestinians, mostly youth, initiated disturbances that spread across the Gaza Strip and the West Bank. Initially, it was believed that they were sporadic riots that would end soon, but the actual developments brought Israelis to realize that the possibility of a "benign occupation" was no longer even a myth. The unrest included attacking army outposts and patrols with rocks and Molotov cocktails, graffiti and the hanging of Palestinian flags, general strikes, and the harassment (or at times assassination) of Israeli collaborators. The uprising caught by surprise not only many Israelis but also the Palestinian leadership in Tunis, its new headquarters after being ousted from Lebanon in 1982.

The harsh measures the IDF used to quell the uprising brought world attention to the conflict, with pictures of Israeli soldiers using batons and tear gas against a civilian population. Consequently, the Intifada also deepened the political rift within Israel between those who demanded a firm hand to put down the uprising and those who argued that advances toward territorial compromise, including negotiations with the PLO, must be made. The military, again, was at the center of the political debate because of its expanded role in the territories. The "Green Line," Israel's pre-1967 border, separating it from the occupied territories, was resurrected as most Israelis began to see the territories as insecure zones that needed to be avoided, and many realized the rising costs – economic, political, and moral – of occupation. A military solution for the uprising seemed unlikely; even the chief of staff, Dan Shomron, stated that it would be "political."

The Palestinian struggle essentially shifted from "outside," led by the PLO, to "inside," where a new local leadership, loyal to Arafat, replaced the elder notables to lead the Intifada. The Intifada brought also important changes to the political organization and goals of the Palestinians, including within the PLO leadership centered in Tunisia. The PLO declaration in 1988 of the establishment of a Palestinian state based on the partition of Mandatory Palestine (according to the UN resolution 181) indicated a new pragmatism. Also, it was the withdrawal of Jordan from the conflict, in its declaration that it has no claims for the West Bank, that forced the PLO to adopt a more moderate position in order to achieve international legitimacy, especially from the USA, as a partner for negotiation. In November 1988 the nineteenth Palestinian National Council, meeting in Algiers, decided to work through political measures to reach an agreement in which Israel would withdraw from all territories captured in 1967. Israel responded with an initiative that included a willingness to negotiate with elected Palestinian leaders from the territories, but not with the PLO, and also reiterated its objection to a Palestinian sovereign state. The Palestinians rejected both conditions, but after accepting the American conditions (the acknowledgment of Israel's right to exist, acceptance of UN resolution 242, and renunciation of terrorism), a dialogue with the USA was opened.

In 1990, however, some of the Palestinians' political achievements encountered setbacks. First, the Intifada seemed in a deadlock as the economic and political costs of the struggle exhausted Palestinian society. Especially significant was the gradual closing of the Israeli labor market the Palestinians depended upon. The mass-based, limited violence struggle was replaced by the escalating involvement of gangs using larger scale and more intensive violence, and the local leadership was gradually replaced by PLO appointees. But the most important change was the decision of the PLO to align with Iraq in the first Gulf War. The Gulf states retaliated by expelling Palestinian workers and canceled financial assistance to the PLO, adding to the dire economic situation in the West Bank and Gaza. Politically, this support for Iraq eroded the diplomatic achievements of the PLO in Western states in general and the USA in particular. Finally, while the PLO retained control of the Intifada, a growing Islamic opposition presented a new challenge.

Toward Peace?

The Gulf War in January 1991, when an international coalition headed by the USA acted to force Iraq to withdraw from Kuwait, placed Israel in the unfamiliar position of being attacked but not retaliating. About forty long-range Scud missiles were fired from Iraq into Israel during the war, and Israelis were equipped with gas masks in case the missiles were carrying chemical weapons. The Israeli military, however, in spite of the missile attacks, remained outside the war because of US concern that its involvement could break up the coalition made up of, among others, Arab states.

In October 1991, in the aftermath of the first Gulf War, the US government initiated a peace conference in Madrid between Israel, its Arab neighbors, and the Palestinians. The Palestinians were represented by the Jordanian government and delegates from the West Bank and Gaza not officially associated with the PLO, with whom the Israeli government refused to negotiate. The Israeli government, led by Yitzhak Shamir, was reluctant to participate in the conference, afraid that it would be pressured into territorial compromises. The US government, however, had the leverage of a loan guarantees request by the Israeli government, which faced mass immigration from the collapsing Soviet Union, to force Israel to participate. While the conference had no practical results, it set the important precedent of negotiations with the Palestinians. Talks between Israel and the Palestinians continued in Washington DC with no significant achievements but, after the 1992 elections, another secret channel of negotiations began operating.

While the talks in Washington continued, and without the knowledge of the participating delegates, secret negotiations were held in Norway between Israeli academics (supported by the deputy foreign minister, Yossi Beilin) and senior members of the PLO. On being informed about the secret talks, the recently elected prime minister, Yitzhak Rabin, agreed to allow the two academics, Ron Pundik and Yair Hirschfeld, to continue their contacts in Oslo, skeptical that the talks would amount to anything. In February and March of 1993 the Israelis and Palestinians in Oslo produced a draft outline of an interim period of self-rule; many of its elements contravened long-standing Israeli policy. In May Rabin and Shimon Peres decided to "upgrade" the Oslo talks and sent Uri Savir, the director-general of the foreign ministry, to head the talks, thus transforming them from academic, exploratory discussions into genuine official negotiations. In August the Palestinian and Israeli representatives agreed on a Declaration of Principles (DOP), and soon afterward the agreement became public.

The DOP agreed upon in Oslo set in motion a peace process based on interim agreements according to which the Palestinians would receive control of parts of the territories, and the major divisive issues – Israeli settlements, Palestinian refugees from 1948, and the status of Jerusalem – were to be determined some five years later. A year later, in October 1994, Israel also signed a peace agreement with Jordan. The DOP's details were finalized in the Cairo Accords of May 1994 which ceded two cities, Jericho and Gaza, to Palestinian control. Another interim agreement in September 1995 expanded the self-government to six major cities in the West Bank, excluding Hebron, and divided the West Bank into "A areas" of self-government (the major cities, about 3 percent of the total West Bank area), "B areas" of joint Israeli–Palestinian responsibility (about 27 percent of Palestinian villages), and "C areas" under exclusive Israeli control.

The Oslo Agreement between Israel and the PLO, signed in 1993, attempted to set forth a peace process that would be based on mutual recognition, coexistence, mutual dignity, and security. The two sides agreed to the establishment of a Palestinian Interim Self-Government Authority for a transitional period not exceeding five years, leading to a permanent settlement and an eventual implementation of Security Council resolutions 242 and 338.[1] Partition seemed to be the logical solution, as it answered both Israel's desire to maintain its Jewish status and Palestinian demands for independence. Three significant obstacles, however, challenged the possibility of partition. First, Israel had since the 1970s been building a system of settlements across the West Bank and Gaza, so by 1993 over 100,000 Israelis were living on the land of what was supposed to be a Palestinian state (see chapter 2). Second, Palestinians who had fled or were deported from Israel in the 1948 war were demanding, for themselves and their progeny, "the right of return" from the refugee camps and other places of habitation to their original homes. And, third, both sides laid uncompromising national and religious claims to the city of Jerusalem.

The core of the agreement was a partition of land and good neighborly relations between Israel and the Palestinians, based on six strategic elements: gradual implementation and evolving negotiations; a shift from unilateral security to security cooperation; advancement of political separation through support of the Palestinian entity; making peace with Jordan; establishment of relations with the countries of the region; and the mobilization of global support. Cooperation between Israelis and Palestinians was difficult. The security demands made by Israel stood in stark contrast to the Palestinians' desire for independence. The Palestinian expectations that the interim agreements would transfer maximal territorial control to the newly established Palestinian Authority clashed with Israeli demands for security. With all its settlements remaining intact until the future final phase of negotiations (and also still growing in size and numbers), Israel's security demands were extensive, including the control of all the major roads of the West Bank. The result was a series of complex agreements that divided the West Bank and Gaza into three different territories. In the "A" areas, the large cities, the Palestinians received full administrative and security

---

[1]   Resolution 242, adopted on November 22, 1967, called for peace based on the withdrawal of Israel from territories occupied in the war and the Arab states' recognition of Israel. Resolution 338, adopted on October 21, 1973, called for a ceasefire in the 1973 war and the implementation of resolution 242.

control. In the "B" areas, villages and rural areas, the Palestinians would have administrative control. In "C" areas, settlements and main roads, Israel would have full control.[2] After the proposed redeployments, the maps showed a patchwork of small and unconnected areas under full Palestinian control, falling far short of Palestinian expectations of sovereignty.

The implementation of the agreements was no less difficult. The Palestinians expected to reach the final status negotiations after most of the West Bank and the Gaza Strip territories had been transferred to their control, while Israel aimed to retain more territories as bargaining-chips for the final status agreement. Israel was concerned with the Palestinian Authority's lack of commitment to combat fundamentalist terrorism and the continuation of inflammatory anti-Israeli propaganda in the Palestinian media and schools. The Palestinians were frustrated by Israeli military checkpoints across the West Bank and Gaza and perceived the continuation of building in the settlements as an Israeli attempt to determine unilaterally the borders of the final agreement. In the three years after the signing of the DOP, relations between Israel and the Palestinians oscillated between periods of intensive negotiations and cycles of violence, with Palestinian suicide bombers blowing themselves up in Israeli town centers and Israeli retaliations that brought the agreement to collapse time and again.

Oslo's Collapse

Tensions were high, not only between Israelis and Palestinians, but also within Israel and among the Palestinians themselves over the fate of the peace process, and events rapidly undermined it. With the difficulties of the peace process, the Palestinian anti-Oslo opposition grew in size and political influence. Islamic movements began to make their mark on Palestinian politics as the Hamas movement established during the Intifada advocated claims made earlier by Muslim activists that not an inch of Palestine should be ceded to Israel or any other non-Muslim

2   The first agreement, signed in Cairo in May 1994, transferred Jericho and large parts of Gaza to the Palestinians and facilitated the return of Arafat from Tunisia and the initial establishment of the Palestinian Authority. The second major agreement, signed in September 1995, transferred more cities to the Palestinian Authority and divided the West Bank into areas A, B, and C. In Hebron, the existence of a small Israeli settlement inside the city led to an agreement, signed in January 1997, which divided the city into H1 areas, under Palestinian control, and H2 areas, under Israeli control, in order to maintain and protect it.

entity. Since its establishment Hamas had built its power base through the establishment of social welfare structures – schools, mosques, youth clubs, and charity organizations – that widened its support from the educated middle class to the dwellers in the refugee camps, enabling it to challenge the PLO. Hamas (together with the smaller Islamic Jihad) waged a campaign of suicide bombings against civilian targets in Israel, often in crowded buses, causing many casualties. In 1994 Israel faced a series of terrorist attacks, the worst being suicide bus bombings in the cities of Hadera and Afula and then in Tel Aviv and Jerusalem. The attacks hurt the Israeli public's sense of security and further eroded support for the peace process. In February 1996, after Israel assassinated a senior Hamas member responsible for many terrorist attacks, a series of suicide attacks was waged against Israeli cities. Between February 25 and March 5 about sixty Israeli civilians were killed in suicide bomb attacks in Jerusalem, Ashkelon, and Tel Aviv.

On February 25, 1994, a Jewish settler entered the Tomb of Patriarchs in Hebron and opened fire on Muslim worshipers praying. Twenty-nine Palestinians were killed and many more wounded. In the riots that followed the massacre another nine Palestinians were killed. The violence of Jewish zealots who opposed the peace process was also directed internally, against the government and its supporters. The opposition described the agreement as a betrayal and the government as disloyal. In November 1995 a young Jewish religious zealot assassinated Prime Minister Yitzhak Rabin after a peace rally in Tel Aviv. This was the culmination of the fierce struggle against the agreement and evidence of the deep schism in Israeli society discussed below.

In 1996, the victory of the right-wing, anti-agreement Likud Party in the elections was indicative of the declining support for the process. Initially, the assassination had created a shock wave that put the blame on the opposition and gave renewed legitimacy to the peace process, perceived as fulfilling the legacy of Rabin. But as the structural difficulties remained intact the change was temporary and two months later, after another Hamas-led terrorist campaign, the levels of support and opposition were the same as they had been prior to the assassination. In the next three years, relations between Israel and the Palestinians deteriorated further. Under American pressure, the newly elected prime minister, Benjamin Netanyahu, signed two agreements (Hebron and Wye) but frustrated Palestinians with demands for "reciprocity," support for settlement activity, and the delay of redeployments.

Back to the Peace Process?

The 1999 victory of the Labor Party, headed by Ehud Barak, changed the momentum again. The new government withdrew the Israeli military from Southern Lebanon, eighteen years after the war of 1982, and entered into peace negotiations with Syria that did not achieve anything. In the summer of 2000, seven years after the signing of DOP, Ehud Barak and Yasser Arafat met at Camp David for crucial talks. Two weeks of negotiations failed to bridge their differences, and the sides departed without reaching an agreement, each blaming the other for the failure of the summit. The official Israeli version, backed by the US administration, of what happened at Camp David blamed the Palestinians for turning down a "generous offer":

> The establishment of a demilitarized Palestinian state on some 92 percent of the West Bank and 100 percent of the Gaza Strip, with some territorial compensation for the Palestinians from pre-1967 Israeli territory; the dismantling of most of the settlements and the concentration of the bulk of the settlers inside the 8 percent of the West Bank to be annexed to Israel; the establishment of the Palestinian capital in East Jerusalem, in which some Arab neighborhoods would become sovereign Palestinian territory and others would enjoy "functional autonomy"; Palestinian sovereignty over half the Old City of Jerusalem (the Muslim and Christian quarters) and "custodianship," though not sovereignty, over the Temple Mount; a return of refugees to the prospective Palestinian state though with no "right of return" to Israel proper; and the organization by the international community of a massive aid program to facilitate the refugee rehabilitation.[3]

While, by Israeli standards, this was an unprecedented proposal, the Palestinian account of the talks was different, and their perception of Israeli intentions was the mirror image of Barak's, as Akram Hanieh, a member of the Palestinian delegation, explained:

> In brief, the focus was the three huge settlement blocs in the north, center and south of the West Bank. These were fattened, their area expanded, and they were connected to each other and to Israel by large areas of Palestinian land in such a way as to control Palestinian water resources in the West Bank. Clearly, the Israelis came to Camp

---

[3] Based on an interview with Benny Morris in 2002, "Camp David and After," *New York Review of Books* 49, 10, June 13, 2002.

David not in search of dialogue with a neighbor and partner but to cement the gains from the 1967 war, to restructure and legalize the occupation.[4]

Some progress was made in the talks on territorial questions but the negotiations failed to resolve the unbridgeable issues that were deferred in 1993, especially the status of Jerusalem and the Temple Mount/Haram al-Sharif and the right of return of the Palestinian refugees. The two leaders also entered the negotiations with internal political difficulties that made compromises all the more difficult. Arafat was undermined by Hamas and the frustration of the Palestinians, whose economic and political situation had deteriorated in recent years. Barak's broad coalition, constructed after the election, fell apart before the summit, leaving him with, at best, a thin majority in parliament. Most significantly, the summit revealed how far apart Israelis and Palestinians remained seven years after Oslo.

The Palestinian frustrations of the previous seven years exploded after a visit by the Israeli opposition leader, Ariel Sharon, to the Temple Mount in Jerusalem – believed to be the site of the Jewish Temple and also one of the holiest sites for Islam and a national symbol for the Palestinians – meant to demonstrate Israel's sovereignty over the site. The subsequent clashes between Israeli security forces and Palestinians escalated into unprecedented levels of violence, destroying the peace process, starting the second Intifada, and, shortly afterwards, ending Barak's term in office.

Unilateralism

The collapse of the peace process and the conclusion of the Israeli political elite that compromise was impossible led to the idea of "unilateral disengagement" as a new and a popular solution to the conflict. The idea of a unilateral withdrawal from the occupied territories, leaving the Palestinians to their own fate and setting the borders to suit Israel, emerged in the early stage of the process as a fallback position. A fence between Israel and the Palestinians was presented as a security measure Israel could or should use unilaterally, should the Palestinians fail to cooperate. Thus, the Labor Party in the 1996 campaign, with

---

[4] Akram Hanieh, "The Camp David Papers," *Journal of Palestine Studies* 30, 2 (2001), pp. 75–97.

its back against the wall as the peace process degenerated into another cycle of violence, used the slogan "We are here, they are there, a fence in between" in its campaign.

In the summer of 2002 the Likud government, headed by Ariel Sharon, decided on the construction of a physical barrier, consisting of a network of fences and concrete walls, between Israel and the Palestinian territories. The growing numbers of Israeli casualties from suicide bombers infiltrating Israel from the West Bank and increased public pressure for security caused the government to support the construction of the barrier it had previously opposed. We will return to the internal developments that led to its construction in chapter 6 and will expand on its implications in chapter 5. This unilateral measure, it is important to note at this stage, received no support from the Palestinians. Palestinian protests received international support, including from the International Court of Justice, which ruled against the fence. Domestic and international pressure caused Israel to change some of the barrier's route, but the project continued.

The disengagement plan from Gaza was the continuation of the unilateral strategy and an attempt to reduce friction points between Israelis and Palestinians. Israel removed some twenty settlements from the Gaza Strip (and also four from the north of the West Bank), relocated 10,000 settlers within Israel, and repositioned the army along the international border. The popularity of the unilateral strategy waned significantly in 2006 as it failed to deliver the hoped-for results. First, clashes along the Gaza border continued, with shelling of Israeli towns and villages by mortars from Gaza and retaliation by the Israeli army. Second, six years after its withdrawal from Lebanon, Israel found itself in another war. Thus, in October 2006, plans for further redeployments were shelved.

The unresolved Israeli–Palestinian conflict is an essential part of the debate over Israel's borders and, consequently, it is difficult, if not impossible, to distinguish between the external and internal dimensions of Israeli politics and society as they continuously re-shape each other. The conflict not only underscores Israel's most acute cleavage – between hawks and doves – but is embedded in almost all other divisions as distance from and involvement in the conflict defines hierarchies of citizenship and belonging. The debate, as the cleavages discussed below and the following chapters demonstrate, is not just about the external geographical borders but also about the internal boundaries, related, in turn, to the dual commitment of a "Jewish and democratic state." The divisions, therefore, unfold into critical questions of belonging and, consequently, practical questions of policymaking, from definitions of rights of entry and citizenship to social and economic rights.

The Internal Dimension: Overlapping Cleavages

The "Ideological Cleavage": Land for Peace?

The 1967 war between Israel and its neighboring Arab countries (Egypt, Syria, and Jordan) ended with decisive military victory for Israel and new territories it now occupied. Especially significant was the occupation of the West Bank and Gaza, which added a Palestinian population greater than that within Israel, about 750,000 in the West Bank and 400,000 in Gaza. Convening in Khartoum shortly after the 1967 war, Arab states declared their refusal to negotiate with Israel or to recognize its right to exist. Israel, for its part, declared its wish to negotiate and willingness to return territories for peace. A week after the end of the war the cabinet communicated a secret message to the US State Department for transmission to the Arab governments indicating Israel's willingness to sign peace treaties in return for territories with some border adjustments. But in August 1967 the decision was annulled, possibly because of the Arabs' insistence on unconditional withdrawal or because of internal opposition. Five weeks after the war, in July 1967, Israel's deputy prime minister, Yigal Allon, had submitted to the cabinet a plan that Israel maintain control over strategically important areas and return the populated areas to Jordan. The cabinet chose to delay the decision and to keep all options open.

Despite the declaration of the Israeli government after the war that Israel had no intention of expanding its territorial boundaries, the temporary occupation became entrenched. Not only were the newly occupied territories valued strategically but their religious and sentimental value was also popularized. Government policies, which opened the Israeli market to Palestinian laborers from the occupied territories and made the Israeli currency legal tender in the West Bank, created a relation of dependency between the Palestinians living in the occupied territories and Israel. More important, the gradual settlement of Israelis in the occupied territories continuously blurred the boundaries between the territories and the rest of Israel so that they were de facto annexed to Israel. The settlement project will be described briefly below and in detail in chapter 2.

Between 1967 and 1977 the settlement of the territories was gradual, with the Israeli government reluctant to allow Jewish settlement in heavily populated Palestinian areas. Settlement policy was limited to small communities in the Jordan valley whose construction was motivated by what was defined as security considerations. But, new extra-parliamentary movements tried to force the government to allow them to settle the occupied territories and make them a part of Israel. For some Israelis the occupation of the old city of Jerusalem, the West Bank, and the rest of the territories was seen as the fulfillment of a divine promise and the establishment of Israel in its "natural" and "promised" (by God) borders. Initially, the Movement for the Greater Land of Israel, established shortly after the 1967 war to influence the government to annex the territories, was made of Labor Party hawks who called for Jewish settlement of the new territories, but soon young Orthodox religious Jews came to dominate the movement.

Early attempts at settlement of the territories by religious-nationalist Jews were sporadic and included the initiative of a small group of Orthodox Jews who in 1968 squatted in the midst of the Arab town of Hebron. The movement gained real momentum, with the formation of Gush Emunim ("bloc of the faithful") in 1974. This movement, consisting of young members of the National Religious Party (NRP), took it upon itself to establish Israeli control over the territories and perceived itself as leader of a national revival that secular Zionism could no longer carry. Between 1974 and 1977 Gush Emunim launched a settlement drive and pressured the government to authorize settlements, even those established without permission. In demographic terms this did not amount to much, as by the beginning of 1977 fewer than four thousand Jews lived in the West Bank, in four settlements, but an important precedent was set.

In 1977, following a victory by the Likud, a party favoring territorial expansion and the retention of the West Bank and Gaza (see chapter 3), the settlement project entered a new stage. Menachem Begin, Israel's new prime minister, was quick to declare his commitment to the territories and stated that "Samaria and Judea [the Jewish name for the West Bank] are an inalienable part of Israel." The Likud embarked on a wide-ranging initiative to institutionalize beliefs in the legitimacy of the new boundaries. Its pattern of Jewish settlement distorted the territories in such a way that any future partition agreement would require the removal of established settlements. The new settlement policy appealed not only to the ideological groups interested in occupying the territories but also to families looking for a better lifestyle: a crowded apartment in the center of Israel could be traded for a subsidized house in a settlement. Between 1978 and 1983 the drastic increase in expenditure on settlements was accompanied by policies in the educational, broadcasting, judicial, and administrative spheres designed to accelerate the disappearance of the Green Line (the pre-1967 border) from the practical life and ordinary language of all Israelis. The pace of settlement increased to the point that in the mid-1980s leading Israeli scholars came to the conclusion that the expansion had made Israeli disengagement from the territories all but impossible.

The fate of the occupied territories following the Likud's victory in the 1981 elections proved that the 1977 elections were not a fluke and underscored the depth of the divide between "right" and "left," signifying not socio-economic perceptions so much as a division between, respectively, hawks and doves in Israeli political discourse. Despite efforts to blur the border between the occupied territories and Israel by either Jewish settlements, roads, and other infrastructure, or the establishment of an ideological hegemonic position regarding the "Greater Israel," the territories remained a deeply divisive issue. Extra-parliamentary pro-peace movements were formed, advocating territorial compromise or "land for peace."

The left–right territorial debate is related to a political philosophy and to wider perceptions of Israel's place in the world. The right adopts a primordialist (and often a religious) national identity, a pessimistic view of a "nation that dwells alone," a perception that a Jewish state can never be safe in the world and, consequently, that territory cannot be compromised. The left, conversely, holds a civic (and often secular) identity and the view of a "nation like all nations" that developed in the formative years of Zionism. This identity translates into a belief that the end of occupation would provide Israel with a "normal" international status and enable its global integration. Overall, position on the left–right debate is the central factor in voting behavior: people support parties mainly according to their position on territorial compromise.

The National Minority

The Jewish–Arab divide has less political impact than the right–left debate but is probably the deepest cleavage in Israeli society. The tensions between Arab citizens and the state reached their peak after the collapse of the Camp David summit in 2000. A series of demonstrations in Israel that followed violent events in the West Bank and Gaza escalated to open violence and resulted in the death of thirteen demonstrators, Arab citizens, killed by the Israeli police. A commission of inquiry established after the events found fault in the police actions but also, and more importantly, found deeper structural causes:

> The events, their exceptional character and their adverse consequences were the result of structural factors that caused an explosive situation among the Arab public in Israel. The state and the elected governments consistently failed to seriously engage with the difficult problems of a large Arab minority within a Jewish state. The government's treatment of the Arab sector was generally of neglect and discrimination. At the same time, not enough was done to enforce the law in the Arab sector . . . as a result of this and of other causes, the Arab sector suffered deep distress evident, among other things, in high levels of poverty, unemployment, shortage of land, problems in the education system and serious deficiencies in infrastructure. All those created ongoing discontent, heightened towards October 2000.[5]

Non-Jews in Israel constitute close to 20 percent of the population or about one million people who belong to three religious communities: Muslim (81 percent), Christian (9 percent), and Druze (10 percent). The Arab citizens of Israel, Muslim and Christian, are a non-dominant, non-assimilating, working-class minority and are considered by the Jewish majority as dissident and enemy affiliated. From the end of the war in 1948 until 1966 the Palestinians in Israel, despite their formal citizenship, were placed under military rule that limited their movement. This policy reflected the perception of the state of the Palestinians as a "fifth column" and had severe long-term implications for the socio-political and economic status of Israel's Palestinian citizens. The very definition of Israel as a "Jewish state" has adverse consequence for Arab citizens, who are relegated to a marginal position,

---

5   The Orr Commission Report, can be found at www.haaretz.com/hasen/pages/ShArt. jhtml?itemNo=335594&contrassID=2&subContrassID=1

politically, socially, and economically. As a collective, Arabs are citizens of a state whose symbols reflect the Jewish majority's culture and are exclusive in nature. The preference of Jews over non-Jews is anchored in laws that deal with immigration, use of state land, and semi-governmental institutions as well as in Israel's basic laws, which anchor the Jewish character of the state. Consequently, unlike cleavages internal to the Jewish population generally perceived as deleterious but also open to change, the national divide is perceived as permanent if not growing. Since 1980, in spite of relatively short periods of optimism, the distance between Jewish and Arab citizens is growing and becoming a major source of concern for Israel's democracy.

More than four hundred Arab villages were destroyed during the 1948 war and more than 80 percent of the Arab/Palestinian population fled or was deported from the territory that later became the State of Israel, and scattered across the Middle East as refugees (see chapter 5). Those who remained found themselves a minority within a newly established Jewish state. For Jewish Israelis, who perceived themselves as a minority in the Middle East and the Arabs as part of a larger Arab nation, the existence of an Arab minority was either undesirable or threatening. From the end of the war until 1966 the Palestinians in Israel, despite the formal citizenship granted to them in line with the democratic commitment of the state, were placed under military rule that limited their movement. The gradual relaxation of Israeli policies toward Arab citizens and the modernization of the rural Arab community in Israel have not narrowed the chasm, but rather highlighted the gaps between the two communities.

Arab citizens are exempt from military service, considered the most significant contribution to the common good and, therefore, cannot count as "good citizens." Because many social rights in Israel are tied to the performance of military service the lower status of Arabs is excused by their non-contribution. Israel's immigration policy also reflected the duality of formal democratic citizenship and a commitment to a Jewish state. Palestinians who fled or were deported in 1948 were prevented from returning while the "law of return" (1950) and the "citizenship law" (1952) granted automatic citizenship to any Jew who chose to immigrate to Israel. Similarly, land policy, to be detailed in chapter 2, favors Jewish settlement. Although Palestinian citizens have the right to vote and to run for office, their political participation and influence is limited. Arab parties are generally considered opposition parties and in spite of Israel's coalition regime they have never been formally included in the ruling coalition. National unity governments, popular since 2000, include only Jewish parties, while Arab parties are de facto excluded from the negotiations and are not considered potential partners.

Personal and economic advancement has also failed to meet the expectations of the Palestinian minority. Education not only offered limited personal advancement as Jews are (formally or informally) preferred, but also created higher expectations and reminded the Arabs of their inferior status and the glass ceiling of the Jewish state. As a result, Arabs lag behind Jews in standard of living, public services, and educational achievements. They suffer from higher poverty levels and unemployment, are concentrated in lower-skill and lower-pay jobs, and are underrepresented in high-skill, bureaucratic, and higher-status employment. While Jews are able to translate their educational achievements to higher status occupations, Arabs find it difficult to do so because of a lack of employment opportunities in Arab towns and villages and discrimination in the job market. Affirmative action initiatives in the past decade, in public services, have so far done little to change the underrepresentation of Arabs.

From a sociological-historical perspective two major developments have been identified among the Arab citizens of Israel. The first, described as "Israelization" or modernization, refers to growing similarities between Arabs and Jews in lifestyle and status desires that translate into attempts to integrate and demands for equality. These demands, however, as described above, are often blocked by the state's commitment to the ethnic Jewish majority. The second development, described as "Palestinization," refers to a growing identification with Palestinians of the occupied territories and the development of an independent, secessionist nationalism. Thus, while "Israelization" would supposedly lead to an Arab identity that is reconciled with the Jewish state and is satisfied with equal rights, "Palestinization" would lead to a demand for recognition and political status of a national minority.

The relations between the Jewish majority and the Arab minority cannot be separated from the wider Israeli–Arab and Israeli–Palestinian conflict. The war in Lebanon (1982) and the Palestinian uprising (1987) contributed to the minority's identification with the Palestinian nation and critique of Israeli policies, but at the same time indicated the political vision of the Palestinian citizens of Israel. While Arab citizens were involved in various acts of anti-occupation protest, the vast majority of action was within the law, acknowledging the difference between them and their brethren across the "Green Line." They have consistently advocated a "two-state" solution, in which they remain citizens of Israel and struggle for equal rights as citizens. The latter is indicative of the Israelization process in which Arabs see themselves as citizens of the state and demand wide reforms, namely annulling its Jewish character, which would allow them to integrate or would provide them with some form of cultural autonomy.

The process of Israelization is limited by the general unwillingness of the Jewish majority to accommodate the Arab minority, religious fundamentalism that ideologically opposes integration, and the persistence of the Israeli–Palestinian conflict. The Jewish majority regards Arabs as potential or actual enemies and as part of the larger Israeli–Arab and Israeli–Palestinian conflict. For the Arab citizens themselves, the conflict, and especially Israeli policy toward the Palestinians, creates a dilemma between their interests as a minority and their commitment to their brethren's plight. Peace between Israel and the Palestinians, it was thought, could enhance the Israelization process, first by ameliorating Israel's security dilemma and, consequently, by encouraging greater acceptance of Arab integration. Second, it could also solve the Arab citizens' moral dilemma, allowing them to concentrate on their community's status within Israel and to reconcile their identity as Israelis and Palestinians. But, with the collapse of the peace process and the eruption of violence, Jewish society has turned "inward," seeking to narrow the differences between Jews through a national common denominator. This became especially trendy after the Rabin assassination, when different initiatives attempted to bring the religious/right and secular/left closer together.

The Kinneret Declaration signed in October 2001 by fifty-six Israelis – secular, traditional, religious, left, and right – received much attention, as Israeli Jews of different affiliations were able to agree on a vision for the state, and it is exemplary for its exclusion of Arabs. The declaration affirmed Israel's commitment to its democratic as well as Jewish character, but Arab citizens were not represented; they were to be addressed at a "later stage." Yael Tamir, one of the founders of Peace Now, a former minister in Barak's government and a philosopher renowned for her work on liberal nationalism (and in 2006 the minister of education in Ehud Olmert's government), explained that the absence of Arabs was difficult but necessary: "I understood that if we begin with Jews and Arabs the break up – not between us and the

Arabs, but between me and the right wing people, among us – will come quickly. We agreed that right after the Kinneret Declaration we would turn to a dialogue with the Arabs."[6]

The demand for equality within Israel and growing identification with the Palestinians of the West Bank and Gaza led to new modes of political expression. First, there is a growing tendency among Arab citizens, especially the younger generation, to define themselves as "Palestinians." Second, religious identity is on the rise and is a new source of political expression added to the Israelization–Palestinization axis. And third, a generational change has occurred as a new generation of Arabs is confident enough to demand their rights as citizens of the state as well as to speak openly of their relation to the Palestinians in the occupied territories and the Arab world in general. This gradual change has manifested itself not only in new Arab political parties but also in non-governmental organizations and academia. New political expressions include protests (in Israel and the occupied territories) based on human rights discourse, attempts to use the courts in equality struggles, and a critical examination of Israel's democratic regime.

Between Religious and Secular

Among Jewish Israelis there is a broad consensus that Israel should be a "Jewish state," but deep controversies exist over the meaning of the term, from a secular perception of a Jewish culture and nation to an Orthodox vision of a theocracy. While church and state in Israel are not separated there is a constant struggle over the boundaries of public and private. In practice, these disagreements translate into different questions over the role of *halacha*, Jewish religious law, in the conduct of everyday life. These questions include, among others, the observance of Sabbath, the import and sale of non-kosher foods, the right to civil marriage, and the conscription of Ultra-Orthodox Jews into the army. Social, economic, political, and demographic changes since 1980 have made these questions ever more acute.

Since the early period of Zionism the controversy over the status of religion has been conducted under the threat of an internal breakup. The potential conflict between the dominant secular and the minority religious groups in the pre-state and early state period was mostly

---

[6]   Vered Levi-Barzilai, "In Tiberias we defined the Jewish State," *Haaretz* January 4, 2002 (translated from Hebrew).

avoided by a series of concessions, trade-offs, and deferral of issues that threatened to tear apart the delicate consensus and pragmatic agreements that in the early years of statehood came to be known as the "status quo." In essence the status quo was an arrangement based on the "freezing" of early agreements and understandings between religious and secular and new compromises of the same spirit. Thus, in the new state it was decided that *kashrut* (Jewish dietary rules) would be observed in public institutions, the Sabbath would be respected, Ultra-Orthodox men and religious women were to be exempted from army service, and the religious establishment would have a monopoly over issues such as marriage arrangements, conversion to Judaism, and burial. Church and state, therefore, were not separated in Israel so that all citizens, regardless of personal belief, are under the church jurisdiction in significant areas of their personal lives.

While the status quo did not resolve all conflicts, it created some flexible guidelines that acted as a starting-point for negotiations. What was not resolved by the status quo was left to the political pragmatism of the leading secular and religious elites. Essentially, divisive issues were depoliticized either by transferring them to the local-municipal or judicial level, or simply by avoiding decisions. The status quo has left in the hands of the Jewish Orthodoxy the monopoly over significant aspects of public life. Marriage, to take one example, was placed under the jurisdiction of the rabbinate (Muslim and Christian marriages are conducted by their own ministers) so that civil marriage was ruled out. Secularists who refuse to be married by the Orthodoxy can either register their marriages abroad (many couples travel to Cyprus for that purpose) or live together without being officially married.

The division in Israeli society between religious and secular, however, does not conform to a dichotomous divide. Within the setting of Israeli society three major cultural orientations and three major publics, rather than two, can be discerned. Surveys conducted in the 1990s point to the existence of a large middle category (larger than either the "secular" or the "religious") that includes respondents who described themselves as somewhat observant and defined themselves as "traditional" or "non-religious" compared to a minority who defined themselves as "secular" or "religious." The religious–secular divide, as many studies demonstrate, is a continuum in which most people select the rituals they participate in and the commandments they obey. At the extremes, the Haredi or Ultra-Orthodox groups tend to isolate themselves from the rest of society and strictly observe the commandments.

For most other Jewish Israelis a bricolage of beliefs, identities, and practices can be observed. Jews who visit shopping malls on Sabbath, a secular practice that defies a religious commandment, will often decline to define themselves as "secular" and are very likely to obey other commandments, *kashrut* observance, for example.

But, in spite of the middle category, the religious–secular status quo seems in recent years to have been crumbling under new pressures. In the Israeli parliament a steady growth can be observed in the power of both Haredi (Jewish Orthodox) parties and an opposing ideologically militant secular camp. Political and public debates over the questions of conscription of religious Jews, gay rights, the sale of non-kosher food, and commercial activity on Saturday are all part of a growing religious–secular struggle that seems to defy any attempt to find new compromises. The polarization is also reflected in the public's opinion of religious–secular relations. In recent surveys a majority of respondents described the relationship between religious and secular as negative and as a great threat to Israeli democracy.

The exemption of Ultra-Orthodox men from military service has been a major point of contention in recent years, often exacerbated by secular and religious politicians. In 1948, David Ben-Gurion, Israel's first prime minister, agreed to exempt Orthodox yeshiva students from conscription imposed on the rest of Jewish society. The exemption was the result, on the one hand, of political considerations and, on the other, of Ben-Gurion's sympathy for the Orthodox community's demand to rehabilitate the yeshiva world after the Holocaust. Initially, the exemption was for 400 students, but by the 1990s the numbers had reached 30,000. The exemption was never formally legislated. Rather, the minister of defense uses his authority to "postpone" the conscription of yeshiva students. From the 1980s various activists began to protest what they described as "discriminatory practices" and demanded the annulment of the exemption. In 1999 the government appointed a committee to find a practical solution to the problem after the Supreme Court ruled the exemption process inappropriate. The committee's recommendations, legislated by the Knesset (Israeli parliament), which attempted to limit the number of exemptions and encourage the Orthodox to join the army, were largely unimplemented.

The commitment of the Ultra-Orthodox to the yeshiva, on the one hand, and the possibility that if they are not in the yeshiva they will be drafted into the army, on the other, also has economic consequences.

The Ultra-Orthodox have a low participation rate in the workforce (see chapter 4) and are the poorest sector in Israeli society after the Arabs, with large families relying on state support. Consequently, questions of welfare and child support are at the heart of the religious parties' agenda. The other, no less important, component of the agenda is a struggle to preserve the status quo against the challenges that are rapidly eroding it.

The status quo is challenged by four interrelated changes. First, the rise of an ideologically liberal secularism aimed at church–state separation and the protection and creation of civil rights. A growing number of Israelis are no longer satisfied with the limitations of the status quo and its implications for different groups. This dissatisfaction is translated into different struggles against the Orthodox monopoly, including demands for civil marriage, gender equality, amendment of the citizenship law (and the religious Orthodox definition of "who is a Jew"), and recognition of Reform and Conservative Judaism. This struggle is reflected not only in the political arena and in the rise of secular civil society organizations but also in personal decisions of secularists to marry outside Israel or to raise a family without formal marriage.

The second challenge comes from the mass immigration from the former Soviet Union (FSU) since the early 1990s, to be detailed in chapter 2. Not only are a large number of the immigrants not considered Jewish by Orthodox definition (born to a Jewish mother or "properly" converted) but many of them enjoy a secular lifestyle (or even an explicitly non-Jewish lifestyle) that creates new demands that defy the status quo. A large number of immigrants and their descendents who are not considered Jewish cannot marry in Israel (which has no civil marriage) unless they go through an Orthodox conversion. Their demand for non-kosher food has led to the establishment of supermarkets and delicatessens that cater specifically for the tastes of immigrants, to the dismay of many religious Jews. These commercial institutions also satisfy the demands of many secular Israelis whose leisure and consumption patterns no longer conform to the status quo.

Thus, the third significant challenge to the status quo is the development of a consumer society. Commercial activity on the Sabbath is a striking example of the crumbling status quo and of the growing insignificance of formal rules (see chapter 6). The observance of the Sabbath was always a major issue of contention between religious and secular that the status quo arrangements were previously able to contain. For the religious, Sabbath observance that includes prohibition of business, commercial activities, travel, and many leisure activities was of cardinal significance. These differences were resolved by informal agreements and local arrangements between religious and secular or, at times, brought to the Israeli Supreme Court for adjudication. But, with the rapid globalization of Israeli society, which transformed patterns of consumption and leisure, the tacit agreements described above were gradually eroded as the "everyday life" of Israelis became more and more secular and rules and laws of the status quo were perceived by many secularists as more and more alien and intrusive. In practice, therefore, more and more commercial establishments, mostly on the outskirts of towns, are operating on the Sabbath.

The fourth challenge to the status quo is the linkage that developed between the religious–secular and the ideological cleavage described above. After 1967 the National Religious Party, (NRP), which previously held a moderate position regarding questions of national security and foreign policy that underscored its alliance with the Labor Party, gradually adopted a hawkish position. This was accompanied by the NRP's leadership of the settlement of the occupied territories and the formation of an extra-parliamentary movement, Gush Emunim. Conversely, the leftist-dovish parties and extra-parliamentary movements were dominated by secularists. Thus, the religious–secular divide was overlapped by an ideological divide that increased the rift between the sides and made compromise and cooperation all the more difficult.

The Ultra-Orthodox (and non-Zionist) parties who maintained some distance from the ideological debate found themselves in a new position in the 1980s. As right and left remained deadlocked the Ultra-Orthodox gained power in coalition bargaining that enabled them, among other things, to receive state funding for their educational institutions. The rise of Shas, an Ultra-Orthodox Sephardic (or Mizrachi) party that gained its power from the Jewish lower classes, added to the tensions. Unlike the other Ultra-Orthodox parties, which refrained from taking ministerial positions that would put them in charge of "secular" affairs, Shas has chosen to hold office. This has pitted them, first, against an emerging party representing immigrants from the FSU over the control of the Ministry of Internal Affairs. In the late 1990s a secular-liberal party, Shinuy ("change"), was formed to "liberate Israel from religious control," and the religious–secular debate has turned even more heated with demands to separate church and state, allow secular marriage, and cancel the exemptions from army service given to Ultra-Orthodox men.

Despite socio-demographic and economic changes that have undermined its power, religion (and the religious) remain strong enough so far to protect their own interests and some of the monopolies they hold. But the power of the religious falls short of being able to define the tangible substance of important policy issues. The religious–secular issue remains deadlocked so the basic controversies cannot be resolved constructively and coherently. The secularizing of some aspects of society and state seem beyond the control of the religious as commercial and cultural activity on the Sabbath have become a fact of life, though so far the bulk of activity is concentrated outside city centers in a form of informal compromise. Other issues, however – army service for religious men, civil marriage, and the general demands for church–state separation – are likely to continue to influence secular–religious relations.

Ethnicity

Ethnicity in Israel is usually referred to a division between Ashkenazim (Jews of European descent) and Mizrachim (Middle Eastern and North African Jews, sometimes referred to as Sepharadim or Oriental). Another, more recent, division is between veteran Israelis and the newcomers from the FSU, who also display the characteristics of an ethnic community. Israel's nation- and state-building ethos negated ethnicity in favor of a common Jewish–Israeli identity that was to override all other identities and affiliations. However, ethnicity gradually came to the fore in different political expressions, some indirect and interlinked with other divisions (religion, class, and voting patterns) and some, in later years, in direct political and social initiatives that challenged the existing order.

The vast majority of Mizrachim immigrated to Israel after its inception in 1948. The new immigrants, who had few connections in the new land (in comparison to Ashkenazi immigrants), and were on average less skilled, also suffered discrimination from the veteran Ashkenazi population, who viewed their culture with disdain. The veteran elite saw itself as leader of a pioneering enterprise that included physical labor, agricultural settlement, and military self-defense. The newcomers after the establishment of the state were to become part of this pioneering ethos in which the veterans already held leading positions. The state and institutions embarked on a project of assimilation that sought to transform the cultural identity of new immigrants but at the same time socially marginalized them, as many of the Mizrachi immigrants either were sent to settle the periphery and/or became manual laborers. The development towns in the periphery were built in the 1950s and (until the immigration from the FSU in the 1990s) the majority of the residents were Mizrachim, who suffered from the limited opportunities these towns afforded in terms of education and occupation. In the early years of statehood an "ethnic gap" was formed between Mizrachim and Ashkenazim, reflected in patterns of residency, educational attainment, occupational status, and income distribution.

In the early years of statehood, besides largely failed attempts to form Mizrachi parties and social movements, the majority of Mizrachim voted for the dominant Labor Party; but since 1973 the majority of Mizrachim have voted for the Likud. As an opposition party with a strong nationalist agenda the Likud was able to appeal to the Mizrachim, who were frustrated with their secondary status in Israeli society. It was the Likud's ability to present itself as a representative of the disadvantaged Mizrachim (in spite of its liberal economic orientation) against the hegemony of Mapai that enabled it in 1977 to win the elections and hold office for another fifteen years. The disappointment with the liberal economic policy of the Likud Party and the growing economic gaps led to the formation of Shas, the Mizrachi Orthodox religious political movement that won four seats in the 1984 elections and at its height held seventeen seats in parliament. In addition, NGOs, largely secular and often dovish in their political orientation, have organized to promote social, economic, and cultural justice for Mizrachim. These groups, in a high-profile campaign, successfully challenged in the Supreme Court policies of land allocation that favored descendents of the veteran elite.

The existence of ethnicity is under debate in Israel as it challenges the ethos of the "ingathering of exiles" and Jewish unity. Many Mizrachim have made their way into the middle and upper classes, and intermarriage is high. But the periphery – and especially the development towns, as the following chapter will detail – were still distinctly ethnic, until the arrival of the FSU immigrants in the early 1990s. Studies show that in the mid-1990s differences in educational attainment, income distribution, and status between Ashkenazim and Mizrachim still existed and, according to some studies, had even grown higher. Politically, ethnicity (Ashkenazi and Mizrachi) can explain some voting behavior and is expressed either in the formation of political parties or in civil society organizations.

Immigrants from the FSU who arrived in the 1990s were, unlike the Mizrachim, quick to organize politically and socially, and used their human capital and the relaxation of the state's assimilationist perception to protect their cultural identity. Thus, a "Russian" political party was formed shortly after the mass immigration of about a million people began; cultural institutes and the media provided services, and supermarket chains were erected to serve the Russian taste, including non-kosher products formerly scarce in Israel. While many of the immigrants are not Jewish by the Orthodox definition (estimates are at about 25 percent), most have adopted a Jewish identity in national rather than religious terms. But, because of a strong feeling of cultural superiority, the immigrants insist on preserving their Russian cultural heritage and dictating the terms of their integration into Israeli society. The relative segregation of the Russian immigrants is also influenced by their secularism – and even non-Jewishness – which causes problems over issues of marriage, burial, and other services that are under the jurisdiction of the religious Orthodoxy. Overall, Russian Jews hold hawkish, economically liberal, and secularist opinions together with an ethnic identity that keeps them connected to, yet separated from, the veteran society.

The Hidden Divisions: Gender and Class

While gender and class are important categories in Israeli society – as gaps between men and women and rich and poor demonstrate – their political significance is relatively small. The context of a national struggle, as well as the relative significance of other cleavages that cut across ethnicity and gender, relegate gender and class interests and identity to a lower status. Accordingly, voting patterns (and party formations) are determined by national, ideological (left–right), religious, and ethnic identities. Thus, different parties (Arab, religious) represent lower-class interests many times in the form of specific sector demands rather than universal class demands. Women's needs and interests, on the other hand, are often neglected in favor of other issues.

Since the 1950s the formal status of women in Israel has been advanced through different pieces of legislation that awarded equality to women, but in practice gaps between men and women in various aspects remained large in comparison to Western democracies. Women still earn less than men, are concentrated in professions that pay less, and are underrepresented in the top echelons of the economy and politics. The national struggle and the demographic concern of Jewish Israelis emphasized family values, and reproduction has confined women to a supportive role, secondary to men, who shouldered the burden of fighting. These gendered roles within the context of a national struggle have provided the excuse for the marginal status of women in the economic and political realm. Other important factors in the status of women are the church–state arrangements and the monopoly of the Orthodox rabbinate over issues of marriage and divorce. Because no civil marriage (or any non-Orthodox marriage) is possible in Israel, marriage remains a religious institution that favors men. In recent years, however, more and more couples have chosen alternative arrangements, either marrying abroad or living together without official marriage. To this one also must add the growing number of "alternative families" that underscore new arrangements the state has to recognize.

The participation of women in the workforce grew from 25.6 percent in 1960 to 49.1 percent in 2003 (numbers are lower for Arab women), but they were concentrated in three types of occupation: teaching and nursing; clerical jobs; and services. While in recent years women have moved into occupations hitherto dominated by men they are still underrepresented in most of them. Women have made advances in some areas such as the judiciary (probably because men prefer the private sector) but are underrepresented in the higher ranks of the civil service and academia. In the higher ranks of management, for example, only 10 percent are women, many of them Ashkenazi, and almost none of them are Arabs. Occupational status is also reflected in income differences between men and women; on average, a woman earns 80 percent of a man's wages. In addition, women, mainly because of the unequal gender roles in the family, work more than men in part-time jobs that further increase the earning differentials. Thus, men work an average of forty-three hours a week as opposed to women's thirty-two. This difference has implications not only for income but also for promotion and status.

In politics women are also underrepresented. In 2004 only 15 percent of the members of parliament were women and only 13 percent of the government, the highest numbers ever. Women in Israel rarely hold senior ministerial offices (prime minister, defense, foreign, and economy). Similarly, no woman has ever headed the high-ranking committees in parliament (ironically, the only time in Israel a woman served as prime minister – Golda Meir – there were no other women in the cabinet). In towns and local and regional municipalities the situation is similar, as only 12 percent of local council members are women. Only five women have served as town mayors and no woman has served as a mayor of any of the major cities.

Women in Israel have made some advances in the past years, especially in a wide range of laws relating to discrimination, sexual harassment, and affirmative action. But in spite of those advances women have retained their secondary status in politics and economics. Many of the issues that are of concern to women are entangled in other issues – for example, the status of women in marriage and divorce – and difficult to resolve in a contemporary political setting. Overall, the combination of continuous warfare, non-separation of church and state, and overarching national, ethnic, and religious divides have made effective political organization of women difficult and have consigned the gender issue to political obscurity. Moreover, the advancements made so far are not distributed equally and parallel other divisions in society, so they have benefited mostly Jewish, Ashkenazi, and middle-class women.

Class and the class divide seem to be affected by similar factors to gender – growing income disparities unmatched by political mobilization. Researchers have found that since the establishment of the state inequality in the distribution of income and property has increased considerably, while consciousness of class differences has decreased. From being one of the most egalitarian countries of the world, the Israeli economy has since 1980 been moving from a state-led and welfare-oriented toward a capitalist free-market economy, with growing gaps between rich and poor (see chapter 4). The trends that began in the 1970s have been strengthened since the 1980s with the decline of agriculture, the rise of services, and the creation of a proletariat based, first, on day laborers from the occupied territories and, later, on imported foreign workers. Indexes of economic inequality began to resemble the distribution in other capitalist states. This cleavage, as mentioned before, is embedded in others and therefore, on its own, has little political salience. When class tensions and disturbances occurred in the 1950s and 1970s they were overshadowed by ethnic protest. The correlation between class, nationality, ethnicity, and religiosity, on the one hand, undermines the possibility of a coherent class struggle but, on the other, economic inequality strengthens other cleavages and is expressed through them. Overall, the economic debate in general receded from the 1970s as both major parties became committed to market economics. This briefly changed in the 2006 elections when the Labor Party's election platform advocated a social democratic position.

Summary

The cleavages described above overlap in various degrees and are reflected in political affiliations and voting patterns. Commitment to democracy, a pro-peace attitude (doves), and a feeling of security are associated with the middle classes, while intolerance, xenophobia, and insecurity are more common among the relatively poor sectors. Also, secularism was found to be strongly correlated with tolerance and a preference for democratic over nationalist values. Ashkenazim tend to be more secular, and are proportionally overrepresented in the middle and higher classes, and among the supporters of the left-wing parties. Mizrachim tend to be more traditional and are overrepresented in the lower classes. Because ethnicity is related to religiosity and class it is also related to ideological preferences. Since the 1970s ethnicity has been identified with voting patterns. The Likud, the large and moderate right-wing party, enjoys strong support from Mizrachim, who carry deep animosity towards the Labor Party, which they perceive as responsible for their absorption and their peripheral status. Both of the extra-parliamentary movements, Gush Emunim and Peace Now, are dominated by middle-class Ashkenazim. But while the right tends to benefit from the support of Mizrachim, who associate with the Likud, the left is predominantly secular Ashkenazi and middle class, on the one hand, and Arab citizens, on the other. The interrelations of the "Jewish" cleavages, and even more so the attempts to bridge them, tend to exclude the Arab citizens and marginalize them economically and politically.

Beyond the political significance of this there is a wider, overarching development of a multicultural society in Israel, divided nationally, religiously, and ethnically. Nationally, an Arab minority is growing into a national minority and claiming not only economic equality, being relatively deprived of resources, but also political recognition, which challenges the foundations of the state. Religiously, secular groups challenge the status quo in various ways and religious group struggle to protect it. And ethnically, a large bloc of immigrants from the FSU is able to resist assimilation and hold onto its traditions, while other ethnic groups also demand cultural recognition. As these struggles clash or interrelate on different planes they present formidable challenges to existing democratic institutions, if not the state itself.

Further Reading

Bar-On, Mordechai 1996. *In Pursuit of Peace*. Washington DC: United States Institute of Peace

Ben-Porat, Guy 2006. *Global Liberalism, Local Populism: Peace and Conflict in Israel/Palestine and Northern Ireland*. Syracuse, NY: Syracuse University Press

Berkovitch, Nitza 1997. "Motherhood as a national mission: the construction of womanhood in the legal discourse in Israel," *Woman's Studies International Forum* 20, pp. 605–19

Cohen, Asher, and Bernard Susser 2000. *Israel and the Politics of Jewish Identity: the Secular–Religious Impasse*. Baltimore, MD: Johns Hopkins University Press

Cohen, Yinon, and Yitchak Haberfeld 1998. "Second-generation Jewish immigrants in Israel: have the earning gaps in schooling and earnings declined?" *Ethnic and Racial Studies* 21, 3, pp. 507–28

Horowitz, Dan and Moshe, Lissak 1989. *Trouble in Utopia: the Overburdened Polity of Israel*. Albany: State University of New York Press

Kimmerling, B., and Joel Migdal 1993. *Palestinians: the Making of a People*. New York: The Free Press

Liebman, Charles, and Eliezer Don-Yehia 1984. *Religion and Politics in Israel*. Bloomington: Indiana University Press

Rouhana, Nadim 1998. "Israel and its Arab citizens: predicaments in the relationship between ethnic states and ethnonational minorities," *Third World Quarterly* 19, 2, pp. 277–96

Shafir, Gershon, and Yoav Peled (eds.) 2000. *The New Israel: Peacemaking and Liberalization*. New York: Westview Press

Shafir, Gershon, and Yoav Peled 2002. *Being Israeli*. New York: Cambridge University Press

Smooha, Sami 1992. *Arabs and Jews in Israel*, vol. II. Boulder and London: Westview Press

2

Geography and Demography: Spatial Transformations

Erez Tzfadia

Twice a year, at the Jewish New Year and on Independence Day, the Israeli Bureau of Statistics publishes a "demographic balance of Israel," which presents demographic distributions according to national origin, religion, and gender. These unpretentious announcements usually become the headlines of the news and provoke dozens of articles and comments in Israeli newspapers concerning the future ability of Jews to live safely in Israel and in the Middle East. What makes these announcements a source of public debate? The answer is simple: they point to the major cleavage in Israeli society, as they present the demographic balance between Jews and Arabs in Israel (see Table 2.1). The "demographic problem" underscores the contemporary debate among Jews in Israel on the nature of the peace agreement and Israel's future borders (see chapter 1).

The demographic concern consistently occupies the Israeli parliament and also the High Court of Justice. One recent example is the debate over the "Nationality and Entry into Israel Law" (Temporary Order) – usually nicknamed "Citizenship Law." The law, originally adopted on July 31, 2003 by the Israeli parliament, bars West Bank Palestinians from obtaining any residency status or citizenship in Israel, even through marriage to an Israeli citizen, thereby prohibiting Palestinians of the occupied territories from living in Israel with their Arab spouses. The High Court of Justice rejected petitions to abolish the amendment to the law, as it ruled that "The welfare and benefit that the Citizenship Law provides for the security and lives of the residents of Israel overrides the damage the law causes to a few Israeli citizens who married or are due to marry Palestinians, and to those who want to live with their partners in Israel." Overall, the

Table 2.1. Jewish and Arab[a] population distribution in Israel–Palestine, 1533–2000 – rough estimates (including the territories that were occupied by Israel in 1967)

Year	Number (thousands)			Percentage		No. of Jewish immigrants since 1881 (thousands)
	Jewish	Arab	Total[a]	Jewish	Arab	
1533–39	5	151	157	3.2	96.2	
1690–91	2	230	232	0.9	99.1	
1800	7	258	275	2.5	93.8	
1890	43	499	532	8.1	93.8	. .
1914	94	595	689	13.6	86.4	65
1922	84	660	752	11.2	87.8	. .
1931	175	760	1,033	16.9	73.6	. .
1947	630	1,224	1,970	32.0	62.1	548
1960	1,911	1,175	3,111	61.4	37.8	1,533
1967	2,374	1,306	3,716	63.9	35.1	1,823
1975	2,959	1,563	4,568	64.8	34.2	2,123
1985	3,517	2,315	5,908	59.5	39.2	2,322
1995	4,522	3,432	8,112	55.7	42.3	3,068
2000	4,969	4,108	9,310	53.4	44.1	3,398

[a]Including "others": Druze and other small religious minorities, and, since 1990, FSU immigrants who lack religious affiliation. The Druze make up 1.6 percent of Israel's population.

Source: Sergio DellaPergola, "Demography in Israel/Palestine: trends, prospects, policy implications," paper presented at IUSSP XXIV General Population Conference, Salvador de Bahia, August 2001, p. 5.

ongoing commitment of the State of Israel to the status of a Jewish state, supported by a vast majority of Jewish Israelis, underscores not only the policies of immigration and citizenship but also Israel's land policies. Demography provides the logic behind the spatial planning in Israel as it aims to secure the Jewish character of the state.

The Geography of Israel – Physical Setting

Israel is a small, narrow, semi-arid country on the southeastern coast of the Mediterranean Sea. Israel–Palestine's area within boundaries and post-1967 ceasefire lines, including the occupied areas under Palestinian self-government, is 10,840 square miles (27,800 km^2). Israel's pre-1967 area is 8570 square miles (21,800 km^2). Long and narrow in shape, it is some 290 miles (470 km) in length and about 85 miles (135 km) across at the widest point. The country is bordered by

Lebanon to the north, Syria to the northeast, Jordan to the east, Egypt to the southwest, and the Mediterranean Sea to the west.

About 91 percent of Israelis live in urban areas. Many modern towns and cities, blending the old and the new, are built on sites known since antiquity, among them Jerusalem, Safed, Beer-Sheva, Tiberias, and Akko. Others such as Rehovot, Hadera, Petah Tikva, and Rishon Lezion began as agricultural villages in the pre-state era and gradually evolved into major population centers. Development towns such as Carmiel and Kiryat Gat were built in the early years of the state to accommodate the rapid population growth generated by mass immigration, as well as to help distribute the population throughout the country and to promote the territorial project of "Judaization-dispersal" as well as a closely interlocked rural and urban economy by drawing industry and services to previously unpopulated areas. Some of these new towns were built on the ruins of Palestinian towns and villages that were demolished and de-populated during the war in 1948, such as Bet-Sean, Beer-Sheva, and Ashkelon. Other Palestinian towns have been Judaized through the settlement of Jewish immigrants, and today are known as "mixed cities," such as Lydia (Lod), Ramle, and Akko.

Israel's urban geography is based on four urban clusters, recently identified as metropolises: Jerusalem, Tel Aviv, Haifa, and Beer-Sheva. These metropolises contain a large number of local authorities (municipalities and local authorities), as well as regional councils and rural localities that are adjacent to one another and constitute one functional entity that integrates economic, social, and cultural relations within the boundaries of the metropolitan area. The metropolises are named after their core cities – the territory of the primary city serving as the focus of activity for the population of the metropolitan area. Here are some details on each core city.

Jerusalem

Situated in the Judean Hills, Jerusalem is the capital of Israel, the seat of government and the historical, spiritual, and national center of the Jewish people since King David made it the capital of his kingdom some 3000 years ago. Sanctified by religion and tradition, by holy places and houses of worship, it is revered by Jews, Christians, and Muslims over the world. In the last century the city has become a national symbol for Jews and Palestinians, which made the city a frontier for the two national communities. Until 1860 Jerusalem was a walled city made up of four quarters – Jewish, Muslim, Armenian, and Christian. After 1860 the Jewish, Muslim, and Christian communities began to establish, each by its own means, new, segregated neighborhoods outside the walls, forming the nucleus of modern Jerusalem. During three decades of British administration (1917–48), the city gradually changed from a neglected provincial town of the Ottoman Empire (1517–1917) into a metropolis, with many new residential neighborhoods, each reflecting the character of the particular community living there. After the war in 1948 the city was divided (in 1949) under Israeli and Jordanian rule: the western part of the city was Israeli and the eastern part was Jordanian. For the next nineteen years concrete walls and barbed wire sealed off one part from the other.

As a result of the 1967 war, the Jordanian part of the city was occupied and added to the Israeli part. Since then, the municipal borders of the city have been expanded and dozens of new Jewish neighborhoods have been established on both the Jewish western and Arab eastern parts of the city. At the same time Israel has limited the expansion and development of Palestinian neighborhoods. Jerusalem is the locus of demographic notion in the Israeli regime. Today Israel's largest city, it has a population of some 680,000, and the metropolis's population numbers 820,000, among them many Jewish settlers in the occupied territories near Jerusalem. Jerusalem also serves a large number of Palestinians living in the West Bank, though in recent years their entrance to the city has been limited by the separation barrier. Jerusalem is a divided city, with inhabitants representing a mixture of cultures and nationalities, of religiously observant and secular lifestyles. One imported division is based on citizenship status: while all the Jews who live in the eastern new neighborhoods of Jerusalem enjoy full citizenship status, the Palestinian residents have limited status of citizenship: they cannot, for example, vote in national elections.

Tel Aviv-Yafo

A modern city on the Mediterranean coast, Tel Aviv-Yafo is Israel's commercial and financial center as well as the focus of its cultural life. Most industrial organizations have their headquarters there, together with the stock exchange, major newspapers, commercial centers, and publishing houses. The population of Tel Aviv-Yafo was 467,000, and of Tel Aviv metropolis 2,731,000, at the end of 2005. Therefore, Tel Aviv metropolis is the most populated in Israel. Tel Aviv, the first all-Jewish city in modern times, was founded in 1909 as a Jewish suburb of Palestinian Jaffa, one of the oldest urban settlements in the world. In 1934 Tel Aviv was granted municipal status by the British administration, and in 1950, after the war in 1948 and the expulsion of the major part of the Palestinian community, it was renamed Tel Aviv-Yafo, the new municipality absorbing old Jaffa. Though Jaffa and Tel Aviv were united under the same jurisdiction, the two parts remained divided socially, economically, and ethnically: Tel Aviv is inhabited predominantly by upper-middle-class Jews, mostly Ashkenazim, while Jaffa (in addition to its pre-1948 Jewish neighborhoods, which are known today as "south Tel Aviv") is inhabited mostly by lower-class Palestinian Arabs, Mizrachim, and undocumented labor immigrants. In recent decades Jaffa and south Tel Aviv have been involved in "gentrification" projects, in which upper-class Jews have settled in new and revitalized buildings; however, this has often amplified the social and ethnic gaps in these areas.

Haifa

Haifa, on the Mediterranean Sea, rises from the coastline over the slopes of Mount Carmel. It is built on three topographical levels: the lower city, partly on land recovered from the sea, is the commercial center with harbor facilities; the middle level is an older residential area; and the top level consists of rapidly expanding modern neighborhoods with tree-lined streets, parks, and pine woods, overlooking the industrial zones and sandy beaches on the shore of the wide bay below. A major deep-water port, Haifa is a focus of international trade and commerce. It also serves as the administrative center of northern Israel. At the end of the year 2005 the city's population numbered 268,300, and the metropolis's population numbered 1,046,000. During three decades of British administration (1917–48), the city was populated by two main communities: Palestinian and Jewish. After the war in 1948 only a segment of Palestinians remained in the city, living in the lower city. The middle level is inhabited mostly by immigrant Jewish communities, mainly FSU immigrants and Mizrachim, and the upper level mostly by upper-middle-class Ashkenazi Jews.

Beer-Sheva

Beer-Sheva, in the northern Negev, is located at the intersection of routes leading to the Dead Sea and Eilat. It is a new city built in close proximity to an Ottoman town, which served as an administrative site of the Negev desert. The city was occupied by the Israeli army in 1948 and has become a Jewish city. Nevertheless, the city has remained a center for both Jews and Arab Bedouins living in the Negev. Called, for this reason, the "Capital of the Negev," Beer-Sheva is an administrative and economic center, with regional government offices and institutions of health, education, and culture which serve all of southern Israel and a population numbering 545,000 (at the end of 2005) in Israel's southern metropolis. Among them 200,000 live in the city of Beer-Sheva. The great majority of the city's inhabitants are Mizrachi immigrants who were settled in the city during the 1950s and 1960s and their descendants, as well as FSU immigrants, accounting for 30 percent of the city's population, who were offered low-cost dwellings during the 1990s. Among the four metropolises, Beer-Sheva suffers from a gloomy image and relatively low economic achievements.

Rural Areas

Within less than a century, the Zionist movement and the State of Israel have established more than 1000 new settlements, such as cities, kibutzim, moshavim, and yishuvim kehilatiym. Israel has a higher ratio of settlements per capita of its population than any other country in the world. The logic behind this, is both political and economic. About 9 percent of Israel's population lives in rural areas, in villages and two unique cooperative frameworks, the kibbutz and the moshav, which were developed in the country in the early part of the twentieth century. However, most of the employees living in the rural areas are not employed in agriculture. This means that to some extent the rural areas in Israel serve as the suburbs of the four Israeli metropolises. Administratively, the rural areas are organized by regional councils, which are each responsible for a number of rural villages.

The kibbutz is a self-contained social and economic unit in which decisions are taken by its Jewish members, and property and means of production are communally owned. Today 1.8 percent of the population in Israel lives in 268 kibbutzim. Members are assigned work in different branches of the kibbutz economy. Traditionally the backbone of Israel's agriculture, kibbutzim are now increasingly engaged in industry, tourism, services, and real-estate businesses. As a result of economic and social crises, many of the kibbutzim today are "privatizing," downsizing their communal institutions and assets, and turning into less communal entities or into a "community settlement" (see below).

The moshav is a Jewish rural settlement in which each family maintains its own farm and household. In the past cooperation extended to purchasing and marketing; today moshav farmers have chosen to be more economically independent. The 452 moshavim account for some 3 percent of the population and supply much of Israel's agricultural produce. Nearly all the moshavim were built after the war in 1948 over the ruins of Palestinian villages. The settlement project of the moshavim served the demographic goals of Judaizing the Galilee and the Negev, as well as providing food, shelter, and employment to needy Mizrachi immigrants.

The yishuv kehilati (community settlement) is a new form of suburb settlement, established near each of the 124 existing communities in Israel and about 150 communities in the occupied territories – mainly in the West Bank – and each consisting of hundreds of families. Each family's economic life is completely independent and most members work outside the community. In the last three decades the yishuv kehilati has become the most popular settlement of the Judaizing frontier and internal frontier regions in Israel–Palestine.

Villages of various sizes are inhabited mainly by Arabs and Druze. Land and houses are privately owned, and farmers cultivate and market their crops on an individual basis. Many Arab villages have grown dramatically since 1948, because many "Present Absentees," or internal Palestinian refugees, were coercively settled in them during the 1948 war. Because of their size they are hardly villages any more, but for political reasons most have never been recognized as cities and, as a result, they suffer from limited infrastructure. Bedouin Arabs (estimated at 170,000 people), a minority within the Arab sector, currently live in two major types of settlements – townships in the metropolis of Beer-Sheva, which are considered the poorest settlements in Israel, and forty-five villages that have never been recognized by the State of Israel and therefore lack basic services.

Demography: Immigration and Absorption

Palestine's partition plan, approved by the UN in 1947, suggested the creation of six areas that matched the demographic reality – three with a Jewish majority and three with an Arab majority – plus the Jerusalem–Bethlehem area intended as a *corpus separatum* under UN tutorship. Following the war of 1948, declared by the Arabs who rejected the plan, the Jewish-Israeli side expanded its territorial jurisdiction at the expense of the Arab side. As a consequence, several enclaves of Arab territory passed under direct Israeli rule and some 200,000 Palestinian-Arabs became Israeli citizens. This new demographic reality, in which Palestinians made up a quarter of the population of the Jewish state, was one of the reasons behind the efforts to bring in and settle a mass wave of Jewish immigration:

> Recognizing the shared fate and the joint struggle for the existence of the Jewish people . . . the Government will act with determination to increase [Jewish] immigration from all countries . . . and create social and economic conditions for a speedy and successful integration of [Jewish] immigrants . . . The Government will put immigration and absorption at the top of its priorities.

This quote, from the Israeli government's declaration in 1996, is similar to all previous governments' guidelines since 1948. Unlike the system in most countries, in Israel the immigration system is nationally selective and actively aimed at Jewish immigration. This system is supported both by the desire of the great majority of the Jews in Israel and by the "Law of Return" (1950) and the "Citizenship Law" (1952), which grant citizenship to Jewish immigrants immediately upon their arrival, guaranteeing them the full legal, civil, and political rights enjoyed by all veteran residents.

The establishment of the State of Israel in 1948 brought with it a large wave of Jewish immigrants from forty-two different countries. Most of these immigrants came from Muslim countries in Asia and North Africa and were known as Mizrachim (meaning "Easterners" or "Orientals"). By the end of 1953, within four and a half years of statehood, Israel's Jewish population had doubled; and by the close of 1956 it had tripled (see Figure 2.1). This wave of immigration enlarged the Jewish majority from 76 percent of the total population in 1948 to 89 percent in 1961. It has also dramatically changed the internal Jewish demographic composition, as in 1948 Jews of European descent (Ashkenazi) were 75 percent of the Jewish population and by 1967

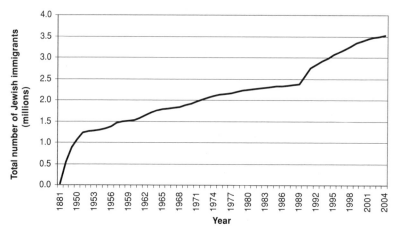

Figure 2.1. Total number of Jewish immigrants since 1881 by year
Source: Central Bureau of Statistics (selected years). *Statistical Yearbook,* Jerusalem: State
of Israel, Ministry of the Interior

Mizrachim constituted a majority, accounting for 55 percent of the
total Jewish population. Thus, while mass immigration was designed
to preserve a Jewish majority, it also underscored the evolving cleavages
within the Jewish society.

The 1967 war produced further territorial and demographic
changes, with the occupation of new territories. Shortly after the war
Israel annexed East Jerusalem and the surrounding territory. Later, in
1981, the Israeli legal jurisdiction was extended to the Golan Heights
(though neither the UN nor any country has recognized the annexation). In the West Bank and Gaza Strip the Israeli administration
did not suspend application of the pre-existing Jordanian or Egyptian legal frameworks in civil matters but placed the local population under military administration. Under these changes tens of thousands of Palestinians in East Jerusalem, and Syrian Druze in the Golan
Heights, earned a special citizenship status, which endowed them civil
rights (except the right to participate in national elections). More significantly, millions of Palestinians became subjects of Israeli military
rule. Israel's settlement policy, which according to some scholars led to
a de facto annexation, resulted in the presence of Jews in the occupied
territories (Table 2.2) and to new concerns over the "demographic
balance" between Jews and Arabs.

Over the years, the State of Israel made tremendous attempts to
encourage Jewish immigration in order to preserve a Jewish majority.

Table 2.2. Jewish[a] and Arab[b] population distribution (1999) in Israel and in the Palestinian territories

Area	Number (thousands)			Percentage		
	Jewish	Arab	Total	Jewish	Arab	Total
Grand total[c]	5,065	4,117	9,182	55.2	44.8	100.0
Total Israel[d]	4,881	1,144	6,025	81.0	19.0	100.0
Pre-1967 borders	4,681	925	5,606	83.5	16.5	100.0
Golan Heights	15	19	34	45.3	54.7	100.0
East Jerusalem	185	200	385	48.0	52.0	100.0
Total Palestinian Territories	184	2,973	3,157	5.8	94.2	100.0
West Bank	178	1,845	2,023	8.8	91.2	100.0
Gaza[e]	6	1,128	1,134	0.6	99.4	100.0

[a] Including non-Jewish members of Jewish households, mainly FSU immigrants without religious affiliation.
[b] Including others: Druze and other small religious minorities.
[c] Including occupied territories.
[d] Including East Jerusalem and the Golan Heights.
[e] Israel withdrew from the Gaza Strip in 2005 and resettled the Jewish settlers within the Israeli borders.
Source: Sergio DellaPergola, "Demography in Israel/Palestine: trends, prospects, policy implications," Paper presented at IUSSP XXIV General Population Conference, Salvador de Bahia, August 2001, p. 8.

A total of 3.5 millions Jews have immigrated to Israel since 1881 (see Figure 2.1 and Table 2.1). In the pre-state period (1881–1948), 547,857 Jews immigrated to Israel–Palestine. Since then, and up until 2004, the State of Israel has absorbed 2,971,827 Jewish immigrants. Together with the several thousands of Jews who lived in the region before 1881 and natural growth rate, this brought the Jewish population in Israel in 2006 to more than 5.5 million, with the great majority of the Israeli population being immigrants or second-generation immigrants. The Arab population in Israel (including East Jerusalem) numbered 900,000 before the war in 1948, 200,000 after the war, and 1.3 million in 2004, owing to natural growth rate. In the past, Jewish emigration from Israel has always been a sensitive issue, not only for demographic reasons but also for moral ones, as it undermined the confidence in the Zionist ethos. For this reason emigrants were described as "Yordim" (literally "descending") or even in harsher derogatory terms. Since the 1980s, however, emigration has become more acceptable and Israelis who "make it" abroad are cultural heroes. In 1981–2001 the number of emigrants was 370,000. Many of them are recently arrived immigrants. During the Al-Aqsa Intifada the number increased, as in previous periods of insecurity, so that the number of Jewish immigrants and emigrants was equal for several months.

As was described in chapter 1, the immigration to Israel resulted in a society stratified nationally, ethnically, and economically. While assimilation promised the inclusion of all Jewish immigrants, in practice mobilization opportunities were limited and often unequal, not only between Jews and Arabs but also between Jews themselves, as Mizrachim were often relegated to the periphery. The national, ethnic, and related class stratification, therefore, is also evident in the geography and settlement policy described below. Into this socio-political and geographic reality of stratification a large wave of immigration arrived in the 1990s.

Immigration from the Former Soviet Union (1989–2000)

Following the collapse of the Soviet Regime, about 890,000 immigrants from the former Soviet Union (FSU) came to Israel between 1989 and 2000. Among them 68,000 decided not to stay and emigrated from Israel. This wave of immigration represents the largest group of immigrants from one country of origin since 1948. Many of the FSU immigrants are not Jews according to Jewish Orthodoxy's rules; although the exact number remains unknown, estimates vary between 35 and 80 percent of the immigrants. Non-Jewish FSU immigrants were granted the status of "Oleh," under the "Law of Return," which guarantees the right of any Jew residing in diaspora to immigrate to Israel and to receive Israeli citizenship automatically. The law also extends to spouses and kin of Jews, who are also granted citizenship though not recognized as Jewish by the Orthodox rabbinate (see chapter 1). The citizenship law is a result of a religious–secular compromise in the 1970s, when it was expected that small numbers of non-Jews could take advantage of Israeli citizenship. The mass immigration from the FSU, including large numbers of non-Jews, undermines the religious–secular status quo but serves two other important goals of the Jewish state. First, this immigration contributes demographically to securing a Jewish (or non-Arab) majority, and, second, its high level of education contributes to economic growth.

The FSU immigrants are highly educated. Nearly 60 percent had post-secondary education, compared with 40 percent of Jews in Israel. The rate of participation in the labor force in the FSU was very high among the immigrants. Of the FSU immigrants, 70 percent were employed prior to immigration. This pattern has been maintained in Israel, and is particularly noteworthy among the more veteran immigrants, who benefited from the employment opportunities that were available in the early 1990s. Those who arrived in the late 1990s – and particularly older immigrants – had greater difficulty finding employment. The unemployment rate among FSU immigrants is higher than among the veteran population. In 1999, 11 percent of men and 13 percent of women from the FSU were unemployed – 40 percent more than the Jewish average, but lower than the Arab average. Unemployment among FSU immigrants has declined as their length of residence in Israel has increased. After ten years of residence in Israel, their unemployment rate was the same as that of the Jews overall. Yet, the gross monthly income of households of FSU immigrants was 40 percent lower than veteran Jewish household's average.

Policymaking and Immigration

Unlike previous waves of immigration, the FSU immigrants arrived in Israel when the market economy was dominant and centralist planning was less significant. With a growing sense of individualism in Israeli social and cultural life, the importance of cultural and social integration diminished. This change in Israeli society redefines one of the fundamental aspirations of Zionism and the State of Israel – "Ingathering of the Jewish exiles" – which also gained the vision of social practice, assimilating the Jewish immigrants into common national and cultural identity. In the 1950s this concept had emphasized mainly cultural dimensions, which were associated with the single melting-pot idea. In the 1990s the concept emphasized mainly territorial dimensions – ingathering Jews in the land of Israel, but not necessarily assimilation. The difficulties of absorbing mass immigration lowered the importance of cultural absorption. Instead, emphasis was put on immigrant absorption within the labor and housing markets.

Consequently, in contrast to the high involvement of the state in the absorption of immigrants in the 1950s, a new policy termed "direct absorption" was employed in the 1990s. Direct absorption retained many of the previous benefits allotted to immigrants but gave them more choice on how to use them. Most significantly, the new policy allocated them money for a year's rental as soon as they arrived, and let them choose where to settle, rather than having this decision made for them. But, when housing costs for both renting and purchasing doubled, and homelessness started to spread, even among non-immigrant Israelis, the government had to intervene. This intervention revived a fundamental aspiration of Zionism and the State of Israel: "Judaization-dispersal."

As a policy toward immigration, "Judaization-dispersal" directed the settlement of immigrants in frontier and internal frontier regions in the name of furthering Jewish control of the entire Israeli territory and especially the peripheral areas, or the "internal frontiers" – Negev and Galilee in Israel, and the West Bank since 1967 – where Jewish settlement was sparse. This policy, discussed below, was accompanied by religious and national symbolism that highlighted, on the one hand, the historical-biblical connection to the land and, on the other hand, the military or security importance of territorial control. Apart from its symbolic role, the internal frontier became, economically and socially, the periphery – the region inhabited largely by Arabs and Mizrachim.

In the early stage of the immigration from the FSU, the immigrants enjoyed the freedom to choose where to settle, but with the rise of housing prices and limited government funding they could no longer afford the coastal area and many had to settle in the periphery, mainly in the Negev and Galilee. As these areas offered limited employment opportunities, the more qualified and educated immigrants found their final destinations at geographical locations where they had a better chance of gaining employment that covered their accommodation expenses. The less qualified and educated immigrants chose their geographical region according to accommodation costs only, and settled therefore mainly in the internal frontier/peripheral regions. As a result, many towns in the peripheral regions, previously dominated by Mizrachim, have "Russian" enclaves, in which the great majority of the population is FSU immigrants and the spoken language is Russian. There are also "Russian" enclaves within the cities in central regions: the immigrants are concentrated in certain neighborhoods, and in some of them they are the largest group of origin.

Community and Politics among the FSU Immigrants

The geographical pattern of isolationism that the practices of "ingathering of the exiles" and "Judaization-dispersal" enforced on the FSU immigrants, albeit in a more limited manner than in the 1950s, drew clear ethnic and cultural boundaries around the new immigrants, on both urban and national scales. Although the immigrants arrived from different parts of the FSU, the majority of them speak Russian, tend to identify themselves as "Russian," and are categorized as such by society at large. The boundaries of the "Russian" category were accepted and reinforced by the establishment of two immigrant, "Russian" political parties, Yisrael b'Aliyah (Israel in Immigration/Ascendance) and Yisrael Beitenu (Israel our Home). The two parties employed "ethnicity" as their main political resource, but still emphasized the affiliation of FSU immigrants to Israel (in the names of the parties, for example). Both parties performed well in national elections during the 1990s, attesting to the success of FSU immigrants in acquiring political power as a distinct group. In addition to taking care of the interests of the FSU immigrant communities, the agendas of the two "Russian" parties identified with right-wing Israeli politics, demonstrating a strong affiliation to and identification with the dominant host Jewish group in Israel.

The municipal elections in the late 1990s and early 2000s found the immigrant community well organized compared with other communities in Israel, with a better understanding of its local interests, better capacity to put forward a strong local leadership, and with the strongest link between the immigrant "father parties" (Yisrael b'Aliyah and Yisrael Beitenu) and their local branches. The political power of the immigrants, at both national and local levels, was translated into the ability to mobilize community resources. For example, an extensive network of Russian media has been established, including four daily newspapers, ten weekly magazines, two national radio stations, seven weekly programs on Israeli television, and four cable channels broadcast from Russia. It took the FSU immigrants less than a decade to regard themselves as part of the Jewish-Israeli nation. Nevertheless, cracks in this adoption can be identified, mainly in relation to the Mizrachim: Orientalism handed down during the Soviet era is carried forward into Israel as a sense of cultural superiority over communities with their roots in Islamic countries, such as the Mizrachim, while at the same time accentuating the ethnic affiliation and cultural identification of the Russian immigrants to the Ashkenazi Jews.

The Al-Aqsa Intifada that began in October 2000 united all segments of the Israeli-Jewish nation, and therefore toned down the sense of superiority among the FSU immigrants toward the Mizrachim and reduced the cleavages within the Jewish society. At the same time, the Intifada drew many FSU immigrants into mainstream Israeli-Jewish society. For example, the IDF (Israeli army) published the information that during the Intifada the percentage of FSU immigrants serving in combat troops had increased, and the percentage of FSU immigrants serving in the army was higher than the Israeli-Jewish average, although no salary is paid to soldiers. Furthermore, the FSU community has been severely hurt by the Palestinian attacks on civil targets, which have generated a sense of partnership with the Jews in Israel. This reality toned down ethnic conflicts between FSU immigrants and other communities in Israel, but built up a wall between the FSU immigrants and the Arab community.

The Ethiopian Wave of Immigration

During the 1980s and 1990s, members of Ethiopia's ancient and isolated black Jewish community also began to make their way to Israel. A secret Israeli rescue mission began in the middle of the 1970s to save Ethiopian Jews from drought and civil war. From November 1984 to January 1985 a forty-five-day airlift dubbed Operation Moses brought 8000 Ethiopian Jews to Israel. It was followed in May 1991 by Operation Solomon, when Israel airlifted the remaining 14,200 Jews out of Ethiopia in thirty-six hours, bringing the population of the Ethiopian Jewish community in Israel to 56,000 people. As with the FSU immigrants, there are relatively large communities of Ethiopian immigrants in several big cities, usually in the very poor neighborhoods. The Ethiopian community has not had the power of the FSU community to organize politically and in general was less qualified to enter the labor force. It is considered to be the poorest among all the Jewish communities in Israel.

The Molding of Israel's Human Geography – Historical Background

"The struggle for redemption of the land is as simple as it sounds – redemption from the hands of foreigners; a struggle to redeem the land from its shackles; a struggle to conquer the land by settling it; and, finally, the most important thing – a struggle to strike roots in the land."[1]

---

[1]   Yosef Weiss, *The Struggle over the Land*. Tel Aviv: Taversky, 1950, p. 10 (in Hebrew).

The molding of the Israeli space during the twentieth century, as a mirror of ideological, social, and economic processes, has been driven by two main logics: first, national logic that was intended to advance the nation- and state-building process by strategically settling Jewish groups to ensure Jewish presence and dominance, and, second, an economic logic associated with a "free-market" economy and individual desires. The latter characterizes the transition from the twentieth century to the twenty-first, namely, globalization and neoliberalism. There is a complex relation between the economic logic and the national logic, which makes them difficult to separate. However, I shall separate them here for analytical reasons. Of course, these logics are not the only ones that influence human geography. There are other logics, such as the environmental one, but their operation is generally brief in duration and relatively limited in influence. Similarly, the chronological division of Israel's demography into three different periods is in reality less clear cut, and other, internal, divisions are possible. However, the transition from each phase to the next, elaborated below, marked a change in the territory and borders of the space under discussion.

In the Absence of Sovereignty, 1882–1948

The national logic was part of the crystallization of the Zionist ideology and goal – to concentrate the Jewish people in the Land of Israel, while cultivating a national-Jewish existence. In other words, the goal had territorial and demographic as well as cultural aspects. The main means of achieving this goal was (and remains) "settlement," which was considerably influenced by the state of the relations and magnitude of the conflict with the native Palestinian population. From 1881 to 1945, the Zionist movement, other Jewish organizations, and private Jewish capital acquired about 8.5 percent of the land in Palestine, or about 629 square miles (1600 km^2). Some 283 new Jewish settlements were established on these territories. Jewish settlement activity triggered local opposition that crystallized into a Palestinian national movement whose opposition to Jewish settlement, geographically speaking, transferred the focus of Palestinian life from Jerusalem to the coastal cities of Haifa and Jaffa. Following the war of 1948 only one state, Israel, remained in the space; the West Bank was in Jordanian hands, the Gaza Strip in Egypt's possession. Most important of all, however, was the "disappearance" of 416 Arab communities and with them about 700,000 Palestinian residents. Most of these communities were

in the coastal area, which was almost completely emptied of Arab villages and settlements, and in the hilly region of the (upper) Jordan
(the Huleh Valley) and the Bet-Sean Valley. All that remained of Arab
society was a small and devastated community, without leadership and
with limited resources.

The Sovereign State, 1948–1989

By 1956 the Jewish community in Israel was triple that of 1948 because
of the immigration wave, only a minority of which came from Europe,
and most from Arab countries in Asia and North Africa. The State
of Israel set up bureaucratic mechanisms that were meant to create a
new, centralized real-estate regime that would promote Jewish dissemination throughout the space. By the end of the process (the 1960s),
the state owned 93 percent of the land. All the land of the Arab
refugees passed into the ownership of the state. More than 60 percent
of the remaining land owned by Arabs was expropriated. Moreover,
Israeli courts determined the legal status of the Negev by defining it
as state land. At the end of this process, it was stipulated in Article 1
of the Basic Law: Israel Lands (1960), that the ownership of real estate
would remain permanently in the hands of the Jewish collective and
its national institutions.

The imbalance in the spatial dispersal of the Jews, along with the
almost unlimited control over the immigrants, set the stage for the
population-dispersal policy – referred to as a policy for a balanced
distribution throughout the country of population, economic activity,
services, and welfare. The population-dispersal policy was and still is
among the most important objectives of the State of Israel, as manifested in the basic goals of all the Israeli governments and in all the
outline plans until National Outline Plan 31 in 1990. This policy
was implemented for the most part by means of the "Sharon plan,"
("Physical Planning in Israel," 1951), named after Aryeh Sharon, the
founder and head of the planning department of the prime minister's
office at that time. The plan depicted the deployment of settlement
as a pyramid, in which five main kinds of settlement would emerge
on a hierarchical basis. Major forms of settlement that were not part
of the settlement network before statehood were urban communities
and medium-size communities of 6,000–60,000 people. These came
to be known as "development towns." This settlement project was
reinforced with hundreds of small, remote, agricultural moshavim.

Some of them, and some of the development towns, were built on the ruins of 350 abandoned Palestinian villages, and were mainly, though not only, populated by Jewish immigrants and refugees from Arab countries, who came to be known as "Mizrachim."

Despite the efforts to disperse the Jewish population, in the early years of the state the urban sector grew. These processes reflected a rise in the Jewish community's standard of living, which was notably evident in the ownership of private cars and the development of a network of roads. Although this network of roads shortened travelling time between employment centers and residential centers, and between the center and the periphery, it was not sufficient to narrow the gaps between the center and the periphery, which in fact were already beginning to widen in the 1960s.

The reduction in journey time between the periphery and the center has contributed greatly to the suburbanization of upper-middle-class Jews to the Galilee and the Negev since the mid-1970s, in what is known as the project of Judaizing those regions. This suburbanization has employed a popular form of settlement known as the yishuv kehilati (community settlement). The linkage between ideological elements and the economic and cultural needs of a Jewish middle-class population helped promote the Zionist settlement project, in contrast to the settlement project of the 1950s, in which poor Jewish immigrants had been transferred coercively to new towns and agricultural moshavim. Thus, the new project of Judaization marks the rise in importance of individualism and economic logic in promoting the national logic. The results of the project, however, are similar to those of earlier waves of settlement: the spatial dissemination of the Jews, so as to adjust the national borders to the state borders.

The accelerated development of community settlements in the Galilee and the Negev (and later in the West Bank) symbolized the deepening of the spatial separation, not only between Jews and Arabs but also between different groups within the Jewish society. The "gray" areas of the law could be exploited to enable the state to prevent Arab citizens from living in community settlements, and communities themselves to select members. The selection process and the relatively high prices made these settlements into Jewish, middle-, and upper-class communities. In addition, many of the projects of community settlements in the Galilee and the Negev came to a large extent at the expense of the Palestinian population, as they were built on land expropriated (or in dispute), were exclusively Jewish, and were not matched by Arab new settlements (see Figure 2.2).

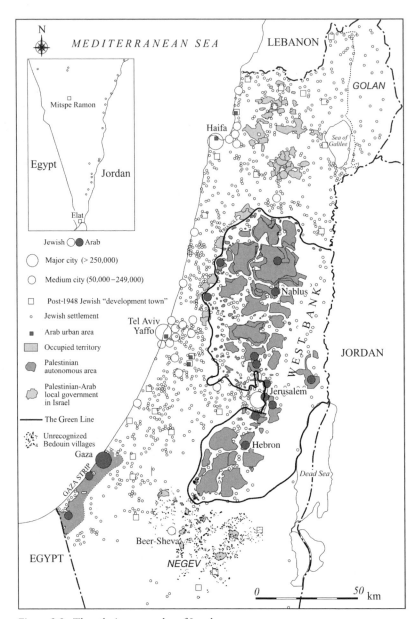

Figure 2.2. The ethnic geography of Israel
Source: Oren Yiftachel, *Ethnocracy: Land and Identity Politics in Israel/Palestine.*
Philadephia: University of Pennsylvania Press, 2006, p. 74

The process of urbanization of the Arab population, which began in the period of the British Mandate, halted and even regressed after the establishment of the state. If on the eve of the 1948 war 35 percent of the Arab population lived in eighteen urban communities and four mixed urban communities, by the end of the war it emerged that 94 percent of the urban Arabs had left the country. Of the Arab population that remained, 83 percent lived in 104 recognized villages. The Arabs who remained in the only two Arab towns and seven mixed Arab–Jewish urban communities were economically and socially devastated, and, together with the village dwellers, were subject to a military regime that restricted their movement. Moreover, the military regime began geographically shuffling the Arab population. Some of them were concentrated in mixed cities, such as Lod and Ramle, and others in Arab villages in the northern part of the country.

Others, mainly the Bedouins living in the southern part of Israel, were transferred in the early 1950s to unsettled parts of the eastern Negev, which later became known as the "restricted zone" or "Sayag zone." The military regime did not bother to provide minimal conditions of sustenance in the form of settlements, and the government did not record the allocation of land to the Bedouins made by its own army, so dozens of "unrecognized" villages emerged in the Negev. Since the early 1970s, for the first time in the history of the state of Israel, seven Bedouin settlements have been created in the Negev, aiming at congregating the Bedouins in "modern" towns.

New Spatial Concept? 1990–2006

The planning doctrine that guided Israel's planning policy for the first forty years of its existence is being replaced by a new planning doctrine, prompted largely by the great wave of immigration from the Soviet Union starting in 1989. New approaches to housing . . . were needed to meet the demands of the sudden influx of some 700,000 new immigrants . . . two other important factors influenced planning policy: the peace agreements with Egypt and Jordan, which changed the geostrategic importance of the peripheral regions of the country, and the . . . globalization of Israel's economy have reduced the capacity of public policy to influence the location of economic activity.[2]

[2]   Arie Shachar, "Reshaping the map of Israel: a new national planning doctrine," *Annals of the American Academy of Political and Social Science*, 555 (1998), p. 209.

This quotation reflects the general consensus among Israeli geographers and planners on the spatial processes that Israel has undergone since the early 1990s: from territorial control to economic globalization and growth, and from Judaization and "frontier settlement" to "urbanization." This change was a result of the social and economic transformations – liberalization and globalization – described in chapter 4 and of the mass immigration from the FSU described above. In 1990 the Israeli government instructed the planning administration to initiate a national plan for immigrant absorption. The result was a five-year National Outline Plan 31 ("TAMA 31"), which resulted in far-reaching implications for the shaping of the country's physical space. TAMA 31 supported the concentration of the population in the existing locations, and the maintenance of green belts between them, instead of initiating new settlement projects. The plan, approved by the government in 1993, was an antithesis to the former spatial doctrine, which was based on the concept of Judaization dispersal and new settlement projects. It seems, therefore, that TAMA 31 was the first planning document which presented a challenge to the national logic and the old spatial doctrine.

This change was continued in the "Integrated National Master Plan for Construction, Development and Preservation – TAMA 35" ("TAMA 35"), approved at the end of 2005 by the government. The overall goal of the plan is, "Development of Israel's space in a way that enables the attainment of the goals of Israeli society, including all of its various groups, and realization of its values as a Jewish state, as a society that absorbs Aliyah [immigration of Jews to Israel] and as a democratic state." Practically, TAMA 35 focuses the development efforts in four main urban clusters (Haifa, Tel Aviv, Jerusalem, and Beer-Sheva), transferring each into a metropolis in addition to attaching the nearby towns and cities, whilst maintaining green belts between the metropolises. In one of the primary versions of TAMA 35, new settlements, as part of suburbanization, were limited because of economic and environmental concerns.

In practice, however, both plans faced the challenges of the new economic liberalism and the older national logic. Many sectors in Israeli society, as well as special interest groups, challenged the plans, and the debate involved politicians and bureaucrats, urban and rural sectors, Jews and Arabs. Furthermore, rapid demographic, political, and economic changes that Israel faced during the 1990s required immediate solutions that TAMA 31 and TAMA 35 did not predict. One of the most important factors that caused a digression from the concept of the new doctrine was an agricultural crisis and the search to compensate the agricultural (Jewish) sector for its shortfall, as is well illustrated in the following quotation from an article called "The End of the Agricultural Season":

> For 120 years, since the beginning of the Zionist immigration waves and perhaps, particularly, since the establishment of the state, agriculture has been associated with the cultural and social essence of growing and developing Israel . . . Wherever one looks, the Israeli ethos is linked to the myth of pioneering settlement and working the land, rural land in general and kibbutz land in particular . . . About fifty years later, virtually nothing remains of this. Israeli agriculture is in its last death throes – economically and culturally . . . It supplies less than 2% of the GNP, exports less than a billion dollars per year, employs less than 2% of the workforce, and even of that total close to 30% are labor migrants. Most of those who persevere in it have to struggle to survive, and are exposed to increasing risks. Agricultural land is indeed the focus of one of today's bitter controversies – which is mostly waged between members of the kibbutzim and moshavim on one side and social organizations and lobbies, primarily Mizrachi, on the other; but hardly anyone argues about giving up the land and converting the orchards to real estate plots; the only question is where the money will go.[3]

TAMA 31 was approved in 1993 but already faced a new challenge of the arrival of 500,000 immigrants. At the end of 1990 the Israeli housing market recorded growing demand and massive price increases, and homelessness started to spread among both Israelis and newcomers. The answer to the housing problem that followed the wave of immigration to Israel during the 1990s became the answer to the economic crisis in agriculture, and accelerated the suburbanization and the creation of mega urban clusters. The agricultural crises that the rural sector faced during the 1980s, led to powerful pressures to change the use of agricultural land into urban land. As the economic and mythic value of agriculture declined, and trends of privatization of wealth and public resources accelerated, members of the kibbutzim

---

[3] Karen Tzuriel-Harari, "The end of the agricultural season," *Globes*, March 8, 2001 (in Hebrew).

and moshavim began to demand rights to public land that in the past had been provided to them for agricultural purposes. Their claims were backed by business people and banks that joined forces with the agricultural lobby in the Knesset. Pressures were added by the economic growth in the 1990s and the desire of middle- and upper-class Israelis for a suburban house with a small plot of land. These trends led to far-reaching changes in land use in Israel. Community settlements, along with affluent neighborhoods in rural areas, commercial and workplace centers were built on agricultural land near moshavim and kibutzimin in the center of the country. The network of roads, which was expanded in the 1980s and 1990s, along with the sharp increase in rates of private vehicle ownership, meant higher mobility for Israelis in general, enhancing the attractiveness of the commercial centers and furthering the suburbanization processes.

The housing crises led the Israeli government to move from total dependence on the private market to direct large-scale construction. This modification was achieved by making more agricultural lands available for new large-scale construction in the internal frontier parts of the Negev and the Galilee. Although the government allowed large-scale building projects that were not subjected to regular laws and even guaranteed entrepreneurs it would purchase all unsold apartments in the internal frontier regions, regions of internal frontiers had limited success in attracting a large population. The high unemployment rate and low wages remained major problems of these regions and many apartments were left empty.

The development of real estate slowed down significantly in the late 1990s owing to, first, the crisis in real estate that almost ended the construction of new neighborhoods in peripheral towns and, second, the cancellation by the Israeli Supreme Court in August 2002 of the decisions that had permitted the construction on agricultural land. In the year 2005 the government approved TAMA 35 but a decade of land transformation resulted in dozens of new neighborhoods. The urban center rapidly encroached on the periphery so as to produce a giant metropolis stretching from Nahariya in the north to Ashkelon in the south, with most of its activity centered between Netanya in the north and Ashdod in the south. This metropolis is characterized by a great concentration of skilled manpower, knowledge-intensive industries, commercial districts, and financial services. The dream of the new plans of four metropolises divided by green belts and agricultural land use, seems to be further away than ever.

The Judaization of Occupied Territories, 1967–2005

The war of June 1967 opened to Israeli society new spaces for settlement in the occupied territories. The national-religious movement of Gush Emunim (see p. 24), was convinced that the 1967 war was an act of God and from the mid-1970s onward made the West Bank the preferred frontier of settlement. National and territorial ideas that characterized Zionism since its inception now combined with messianic ideas to create mechanisms of settlement driven by a religious conception, supported by the government, especially after the political revolution of 1977. In less than twenty years Israeli governments established over 130 community settlements in the occupied territories. In fact, the settlements copied the typical "yishuv kehilati" – the Jewish suburb of the Galilee and the Negev. The "yishuv kehilati" helped many colonists settled in the territories, to realize their dream of a house located on the land yet close to the center of the country, and at a low price thanks to government subsidies and expropriation of lands.

During the 1990s Jewish settlement in the West Bank expanded as Ultra-Orthodox settlements were also established. For the Ultra-Orthodox, one of the poorest sectors in Israel, the new settlements in the West Bank presented a chance for affordable housing in gated Ultra-Orthodox communities. Within two decades the Jewish population in the West Bank had therefore grown from 23,000 settlers in 1984 to 122,000 settlers in 2004. These numbers do not include Jewish residents in the new Jewish neighborhoods in East Jerusalem.

The first and the second Palestinian uprisings (Intifada) (1987–91; 2000–5) proved that the occupation of the territories has a high cost. It was the first Intifada (1987–91) that demonstrated to the Jewish elites, that there is a clash between territorial considerations, which up till then had been relatively cost-free, and economic development. First, the assumption that land could be expropriated and settlements built for a relatively low cost was proven wrong. The defense of the settlements was costly, and services and infrastructure were more expensive because of the security threats. Second, the continuing Israeli–Palestinian struggle over the territories was gradually perceived as limiting Israel's global integration, especially by the economic elites (see chapter 1).

Israeli governments responded to the changes, especially after peace talks with the Palestinians began in 1993, by limiting the numbers of new settlements, whilst still allowing the expansion of existing ones. The settlers, for their part, responded by increasing the numbers of unauthorized outposts and settlements. Those initiatives were over-looked or often supported by the army and government. After the Oslo Agreements, the government withdrew the army from most of the central Palestinian cities but maintained control over the rural areas where settlements are located, and built a large road infrastructure for the settlers, connecting them to the center of Israel.

In the middle of the second Intifada, after massive Palestinian suicide terrorist attacks on Israeli civilians, the Israeli government decided to build a physical barrier in the West Bank, consisting of a network of fences and concrete walls (see Figure 2.3). The barrier separates the Palestinian population from Israeli civilians and settlers. The Israeli government presented the fence as a necessary tool to protect Israeli civilians from Palestinian terrorism but it remains controversial. Resis-tance voiced by human rights organizations in Israel and Palestine claimed that the fence encroached on Palestinian farms, separates farm-ers from their lands, and isolates Palestinian villages. The International Court of Justice also ruled that the barrier is against international law, but construction was not stopped. However, these pressures and the decisions of the Israeli Supreme Court, have led to several changes in the route of the wall, which brought it closer to the "Green Line," the 1967 border. The barrier annexes 75 percent of the Jewish settlers in the West Bank to Israel, as well as all the post-1967 new Jewish neigh-borhoods that have been constructed in East Jerusalem. It seems, from several governmental announcements, that the route of the barrier is envisioned as a future border between Israelis and Palestinians, against the will of the Palestinians.

Toward the End of Demography and Geography?

Over the past 120 years, the Israeli–Palestinian space under Israeli-Jewish-Zionist hegemony has been molded by two main logics, the national one and the economic one. These logics, together and sepa-rately, have created a segregated space, geographically, ethnically, and economically, which is characterized by exclusion and gaps between center and periphery, Arabs and Jews, Mizrachim and Ashkenazim, and Ultra-Orthodox and secular. For decades the Zionist movement, and subsequently the state of Israel, was prepared to invest huge sums

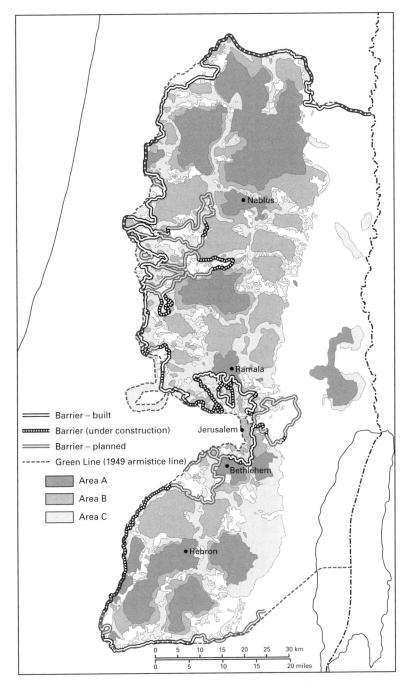

Figure 2.3. The physical barrier in the West Bank, September 2006
Source: B'tselem – The Israeli Information Center for Human Rights in the Occupied
Territories, 2006 (available at www.btselem.org/Download/Separation_Barrier_Map_
Eng.pdf)

in defense, and settlement was considered an aspect of security in the broad sense of the word. This involved not only direct military expenditures, but also expenditures on maintaining and changing the demographic balance between Jews and Arabs in border areas and the internal frontier.

Even if deploying settlement at the periphery lacked economic logic, the state transferred many resources to the peripheral settlements in order to maintain and reinforce territorial and demographic interests. This was especially evident in the territories occupied in 1967 with the large investment designed to erase the "Green Line" and make Israel's presence in the territories a recognized fact. The Palestinian uprising raised the cost of occupation and turned Israel's presence in the territories into a major internal and external dispute. The construction of the separation barrier may be Israel's attempt to unilaterally redraw its external boundaries.

Internally, the new spatial doctrine, presented at TAMA 31 and TAMA 35, intended to limit settlement activity in favor of environmental concerns and long-term planning of space. These plans, however, were challenged by both the national and the economic logics. Suburbanization and community settlements were, on the one hand, driven by the rising lifestyle demand of affluent settlements and spacious housing. On the other hand, these settlements were legitimized by the national logic of settling the periphery and changing the demographic balance between Jews and Arabs.

Further Reading

Alterman, Rachelle 2002. *Planning in the Face of Crisis: Land Use, Housing and Mass Immigration in Israel.* London: Routledge

Kemp, Adriana, David Newman, Uri Ram, and Oren Yiftachel (eds.) 2004. *Israelis in Conflict: Hegemonies, Identities and Challenges.* Brighton: Sussex Academic Press

Kimmerling, Baruch 2001. *The Invention and Decline of Israeliness: State, Society, and the Military.* Berkeley: University of California Press

Lustick, S. I. 1993. *Unsettled States, Disputed Lands.* New York: Cornell University Press

Shafir, Gershon, and Peled Yoav (2002). *Being Israeli.* New York: Cambridge University Press

Yiftachel, Oren 2006. *Ethnocracy: Land and Identity Politics in Israel/Palestine.* Philadelphia: University of Pennsylvania Press

3

The Political System: Government, Parliament, and the Court

Arye Naor

On the eve of the 1980s the State of Israel underwent a profound transformation. The *mahapach* (electoral upheaval) which put Menachem Begin and the Likud movement into power on May 17, 1977 was far more than the first transfer of power to another party since David Ben-Gurion established Israel's first government on May 14, 1948. The political transformation indicated a profound change in the Israeli political system that included, on the one hand, a political tie between two political parties and two ideologies and, on the other hand, growing instability and a governance crisis. Various attempts to stabilize the political system in the past two decades, described below, have largely failed. The political system, far from providing answers to the deep schisms in Israeli society described in previous chapters, seems to be dominated by them.

The *Mahapach* (Electoral Upheaval)

During Israel's first three decades, the Labor movement enjoyed hegemony over politics, economics, culture, and the dominant ideology in Israel. Earlier still, from the middle of the 1930s, the Labor movement had similar hegemony over the World Zionist Organization and the *yishuv*.[1] The Labor movement had also formed the historical narrative of the establishment of Israel, and by excluding the Zionist right wing from the national historical consciousness, had fortified its control all the more. The Party of Workers of Eretz Yisrael (Mifleget Poalei Eretz

---

[1] *Yishuv*, meaning "settlement," was the term for the Jewish community in Eretz Yisrael (the Land of Israel) under British mandate, prior to the establishment of the State of Israel.

Yisrael – Mapai) – the primary group in the Zionist Labor movement – had controlled the axis of the political system: without Mapai it was impossible to establish a government, and Mapai was always the primary ruling party in a coalition structure in which the junior partners came and went. In light of the first signs of weakening in the middle of the 1960s, Mapai had begun to unify the factions of social-democratic Zionism into a common alignment, and had ultimately established a single party: the Labor Party.

On the right, a similar organizational process had begun. The Herut (Liberty) movement and the Liberal Party had established a parliamentary bloc, and in the early 1970s additional bodies had joined them, establishing the Likud Party. At the center of public discourse was the question of the future of the territories that Israel had conquered in the Six Day War (1967). The Labor movement supported negotiation with Arab states, in which the state's borders, on all its frontiers, would be determined through territorial compromise. The Likud placed the idea of *Eretz Yisrael ha'Shlema* ("Greater Israel") – the demand to annex the West Bank and Gaza Strip to Israel – at the top of its election platform, leaving somewhat vague the future of the Sinai peninsula and the Golan Heights, conquered from the Egyptians and Syrians, respectively.

Settlement policy was derived from this ideological schism: Labor believed that Israel should establish settlements in those territories that in the future would be integral parts of the state, and refrain from settling territories that would be returned to Arab control, according to the territorial compromise doctrine. According to Likud's stance, it was necessary to settle everywhere, in order to frustrate territorial compromise, which would mean repartition of the country. It was no coincidence that Begin visited a settlement in Samaria after his election victory, there declaring: "there will be many Elon Morehs." (Elon Moreh was a group of settlers wishing to establish a settlement by the same name, which is the name of the settlement from the time of Abraham near Shechem [Genesis 12:6], in Samaria.) The city of Shechem as it exists today is called Nablus in English, Arabic, and most other languages, and is one of the main Palestinian cities. The establishment of a Jewish settlement bearing the biblical name Elon Moreh proximate to Arab Nablus symbolized the settlers' struggle for the restoration of Jewish rule based on the Bible. That approach fitted Begin's worldview.

The government Begin founded was composed of representatives of Likud, the religious parties (the religious nationalists and
Agudat Yisrael) and the Democratic Movement for Change (haTnuah
haDemocratit l'Shinui, a centrist party that won fifteen Knesset seats
but crumbled away during one term). Begin's rhetoric and the politics
of the religious parties granted the government a quasi-religious character. For example, pursuant to the coalition agreement, the restriction upon the number of yeshiva[2] students exempt from mandatory
military service was revoked. The National Religious Party was also
satisfied. It received the education portfolio. The Labor Party had not,
for ideological reasons, been willing to allow the religious to run the
education system, and the education portfolio had always been in the
hands of a "Labor" minister; yet now the National Religious Party
had an opportunity to affect the curriculum. In the eyes of Prime
Minister Begin, that entailed no concession, as he saw Jewish nationalism as essentially connected to the Jewish religion. Indeed, beyond
the material and symbolic achievements of the religious parties, Begin's
nationalistic rhetoric was also of religious pathos. In presenting his first
government to the Knesset, he said, inter alia:

> The Government of Israel shall not ask any nation, near or far, great
> or small, to recognize our right to exist. We received our right to exist
> from the God of our forefathers at the dawn of human civilization
> nearly four thousand years ago, and for that right, which has been
> sanctified with the blood of Jews from generation to generation,
> we have paid a price unheard of in the history of nations . . . I
> thus reemphasize that we do not expect that it be requested on
> our behalf that our right to exist in the land of our forefathers be
> recognized. Recognition of another sort is needed between us and
> our neighbors: the recognition of sovereignty and the mutual need
> to live in peace and understanding. (Knesset Protocols 80 (1977) 15)

Thus, at one of the climactic moments of his political career, Begin
described the covenant between the pieces (Genesis 15:1–21) as a real
historical event, which took place in time, at the beginning of the
evolution of human civilization, and in which God granted the Jewish people its right of existence in the Land of Israel. Begin's political
theology did not end at the significance of God's single moment of
revelation to Abraham, rather it continued along real history, during

---

[2]   A yeshiva is a place of Jewish religious study.

which persecutions and bloodshed were the lot of the Jews, express-
ing the historic uniqueness of that people. Emphasis of the unprecedented human price the Jewish people paid for its national right is
a reference to the Holocaust, which was a central motif in Begin's
speeches and policy, used as a source and justification for the offensive
security view which would lead him to adopt the "Begin Doctrine"
in Israel's nuclear strategy, according to which the State of Israel will
prevent – even through use of military force – her enemies from suc-
ceeding in their plans to destroy her. It was by force of this doctrine
that in June 1981 the Israeli air force bombed the nuclear reactor built
by Saddam Hussein in Iraq. The justification for the 1982 Lebanon
War was also based on the lessons of the Holocaust, as he understood
and presented them. He saw the Palestinians' leader, Yasser Arafat, as
Hitler's successor, and thus Israel was, in his opinion, permitted to
initiate a military offensive against Arafat and the PLO (Palestine Liberation Organization) that he headed, even though at that time (1982)
Israel had other options as well.

Begin's concept of Jewish history was one of survival. Persecution
of the Jews continued throughout history, a fact adding to the right
deriving from the divine promise a dimension of human moral duty,
owed by the persecuting world to the persecuted Jewish people. The
religious experience and ideology of martyrdom are connected to the
right to be a free people in the land of the forefathers, and that right will
be realized through mutual recognition between Israel and her neighbors. Thus Begin progressed from a theological discussion of history to
the diplomacy of peace, which, with the assistance of the United States,
yielded the peace treaty signed by Israel and Egypt in March 1979, less
than two years after Begin's ascent to power. The peace treaty was based
on the international border between Egypt and mandatory Palestine.
In 1982 Israel evacuated all her forces from the Sinai Peninsula conquered in 1967, and returned it to Egyptian sovereignty. In return,
Israel received a peace treaty with mutual recognition, normalization
agreements, and demilitarization of the area from which the military
threat to Israel had been posed. In the framework of the negotiations
with Egypt and the United States, Israel raised the proposal of autonomy for the Palestinians in the West Bank and Gaza Strip as an interim
arrangement toward resolution of the conflict between the two peo-
ples. That proposal was accepted in the Camp David Accords between
Israel and Egypt, signed by US President Jimmy Carter as a witness
(1978), and was also the basis of the Israel–PLO agreement ("The Oslo

Accords"), signed by US President William Jefferson Clinton (1993).
It was by force of that agreement that the Palestinian Authority was
established, but the process of putting an end to the hundred years'
bloody conflict has not yet been completed.

Economic and Political Instability

Begin's ideology, and the economic and social policy of the Likud governments in the 1980s, were based on liberalization of the economy,
accompanied by massive investment in renovation of poverty-stricken
neighborhoods in large cities and of the development towns which
had been established in the 1950s and 1960s without sufficient economic infrastructure. A special agency was established for the renovation project (Project Renewal), and a fundraising drive was made for
it in financially sound Jewish communities in the West, each of which
adopted a neighborhood in Israel, creating involvement of the donor
community in the life of the recipient community. Most of the renovation was of housing. Funding having been attained and bureaucratic
hurdles removed, the size of many families' apartments, and thus their
standard of living, were increased.

Projects for social and environmental rehabilitation were also under-
taken, but they were less successful than the physical renovation. Likud
governments increased welfare payments through the National Insurance Agency, but the social gap deepened as a result of the reper-
cussions of their economic policies. One of the weak points of the
economic policy was inflation, which, together with the balance of
payments, threatened to topple the economic structure (see pp. 95–7).
It is no wonder that finance ministers were replaced rapidly, as seen in
Table 3.1.

The fast pace of personnel changes in the Finance Ministry contributed to the instability of the political system and expressed a serious
difficulty to govern. Finance ministers were also replaced in quick succession after the stabilization of the economy and the overcoming of
inflation in the mid 1980s. In the twenty-nine years since the *mahapach* (1977–2006) there have been fifteen finance ministers, as opposed
to only five during the first twenty-nine years of the State of Israel
(1948–77). Comparison of the two periods reveals a dimension of
instability, which has been all the more prominent in the decade since
the assassination of Prime Minister Yitzhak Rabin: from 1996 until
2006 there have been eight finance ministers, with an average term

Table 3.1. Finance ministers and the rise and fall in inflation, 1977–86

Year	Annual inflation rate (in percentages)	Finance minister
1977	42.5	Simcha Erlich (June–Dec.)
1978	48.1	Simcha Erlich
1979	111.4	Simcha Erlich (Jan.–Nov.); Yiga'el Horowitz (Nov.–Dec.)
1980	132.9	Yiga'el Horowitz
1981	101.5	Yoram Aridor
1982[a]	131.5	Yoram Aridor
1983	190.7	Yoram Aridor (Jan.–Oct.); Yig'al Cohen-Orgad (Oct.–Dec.)
1984	444.9	Yig'al Cohen-Orgad (Jan.–Sept.); Yitzhak Moda'i (Sept.–Dec.)
1985[b]	185.2	Yitzhak Moda'i
1986	19.7	Yitzhak Moda'i (Jan.–June); Moshe Nisim (June–Dec.)

[a] On June 6, 1982 the Lebanon War ("Operation Peace for Galilee") broke out.
[b] On July 1, 1985 an emergency plan for stabilization of the economy was instated.
Source: The Central Bureau of Statistics.

of a year and a quarter each. During that same period, which overlaps Tony Blair's term as prime minister of the British government, there have been five prime ministers in Israel (Shimon Peres, Benjamin Netanyahu, Ehud Barak, Ariel Sharon, and Ehud Olmert), with an average term of a mere two years each. There have been seven defense ministers in the past decade (Shimon Peres, Yitzhak Mordechai, Moshe Arens, Ehud Barak, Benjamin Ben Eliezer, Shaul Mofaz, and Amir Peretz). The number of justice ministers is even greater – no fewer than nine justice ministers have served since Rabin's assassination. The core of government in Israel has thus found itself in a chronic instability crisis.

Power Shifts

Dramatic failures, as Table 3.2 demonstrates, underscore the transfers of power. By 1977 the fall of the Labor Party could not be detached from the Yom Kippur War (1973), in which Israel was caught by strategic surprise, which prevented her from winning unequivocal military

Table 3.2. Results of the Knesset elections, 1977–2006 (number of Knesset seats)

Year	Likud	Labor	Right including Religious	Left including Arab	Center	Prime ministerial elections (in percentages)[a]
1977	43	32	20	10	15	
1981	48	48	16	4	4	
1984	41	44	20	9	6	
1988	40	39	25	16		
1992	32	44	27	17		
1996	34	32	32	18	4	Netanyahu 50.5 Peres 49.5
1999	19	26	41	22	12	Barak 56.08 Netanyahu 43.92
2001						Sharon 62.39 Barak 37.61
2003	38	19	31	17	15	
2006	12	19	38	15	36	

[a]Direct prime ministerial elections have been held only three times, and the crises which led to the relevant constitutional amendments are discussed below.

Source: Knesset website www.knesset.gov.il.

decision. A legal commission of inquiry headed by Supreme Court President Shimon Agranat dismissed the chief of the IDF general staff and a number of additional generals, but the public did not find that sufficient. Public pressure led to the resignation of Prime Minister Golda Meir and the establishment of the first Rabin government (1974–7). However, the process did not end with the replacement of Labor Party heads, and in 1977 that party lost its political precedence and the Likud rose to power.

A similar process occurred in the years 1982–4. Israel's war against the PLO in Lebanon had become a quagmire; the number of casualties rose, and, as a result of a mishap in the operational liaison with the (then) pro-Israeli militia of the Christian community in Lebanon, that militia was able to commit a massacre of Palestinian civilians living in refugee camps in Beirut (Sabra and Shatila). A commission of inquiry headed by the then Supreme Court President, Yitzhak Kahan, dismissed Defense Minister Ariel Sharon and a number of high-ranking officers, reasoning that because of their failure to predict the tragedy despite all that was known to them about that militia they should bear indirect responsibility for it. Six months later Begin stepped down and went into seclusion; his successor to the Likud leadership, Yitzhak

Shamir, had to ward off an attempt within his own party to undermine his leadership; the economy deteriorated, and inflation reached
impossible dimensions. The elections were advanced because of a
political crisis which also contributed to crystallizing the awareness
of Likud's failure.

The public opinion polls taken prior to and on the morning of the
elections showed that the left wing was headed for a dramatic victory,
and that Shimon Peres was to be the next prime minister. There was
a change, however, at the last moment, and a considerable percentage
of right-wing voters changed their minds and gave their vote to their
old party, despite the dismal record of the past years. The explanation
for that can be found in an understanding of voting patterns in the
eighties and nineties as an expression of personal, family, and group
identity. People's votes did not always reflect their views, and that
cognitive dissonance led to a delay in their arrival at the polls because
of vacillation which continued until the last moment. The result was
a tie. The right-wing bloc had sixty-one seats in the Knesset, but
that number included the single-seat party of Meir Kahana, who was
disqualified from partnership in any government owing to his racist
and anti-democratic positions, and thus the right wing had sixty seats,
the left wing had fifty-nine, and one right-wing seat was disqualified.
That situation forced the central players to establish a rotational national
unity government – during the first two years Labor leader Shimon
Peres was prime minister, and during the next two years the position
was transferred to Likud leader Yitzhak Shamir.

In 1984, 1992, and 1999 elections were held against the backdrop of
the failure of the Likud's policy during the term prior to the elections:
in 1984 elections were held against the backdrop of Begin's resignation,
the Lebanon War, and the inflation crisis; in 1992 elections were held
against the backdrop of the first Intifada and the failure of the right
wing's security policy; in 1999 elections were held against the backdrop
of Benjamin Netanyahu's government's difficulties and his inability to
stabilize his leadership within the government itself, in the Knesset,
and in public opinion. To that should be added the right wing's returns
to power: in 1996 Knesset and prime ministerial elections were held
against the backdrop of the assassination of Yitzhak Rabin on the
one hand, and the failure of the security policy of the left wing on
the other; in 2001 elections were held against the backdrop of the
outbreak of the second Intifada and the failure of Ehud Barak's policy
and leadership.

The Unbroken Tie

Politically, the root of the instability problem was the unbroken tie between the two main parties of the 1980s and 1990s – Likud and Labor, as Table 3.2 shows. The data in the table shows a right turn on the part of the Israeli public. During the thirty years since the 1977 *mahapach*, power has been transferred from Likud to Labor three times (the 2006 elections are not included, as power was transferred from the right to the center, which was fundamentally a faction of the right); however, as it appears from the concentration of data according to blocs, even when the Labor candidate succeeded in establishing a coalition by enjoining part of the right-wing bloc (usually a religious party with a right-wing orientation regarding foreign policy and security, which joined the left-wing coalition since the right-wing was unable to establish a stable coalition), the right wing held approximately 50 percent of the seats in the Knesset.

The unbroken tie was the result of an unresolved ideological struggle between right and left. As mentioned, standing in the center of Israel's political discourse since the Six Day War (1967) was the future of the areas of the West Bank (Judea and Samaria) conquered from Jordan and the Gaza Strip conquered from Egypt (see chapter 1). From the geographical-historical perspective, those areas are parts of historical Eretz Yisrael. It is the land of the Bible, and as Menachem Begin wrote to President Ronald Reagan in 1982, there the kings of ancient Judaea and Israel ruled, and there the prophets of Israel handed down morals for all of humanity. However, those strips of land were also densely populated by Palestinian Arabs. Symbolic components developed in the political discourse beside strategic ones, affected the governability distress and the difficulty in reaching political decisions. The hard-line ideological position toward the territories held by Israel (the "hawkish" position) was that Israeli rule should be preserved there – for security reasons, because of the historic tie, as a secular version of the idea of Greater Israel, or as fulfillment of the divine promise, as per the national religious camp which stood for Greater Israel. On the other hand, the moderate ("dovish") stance toward the territories was that most of them should be conceded for peace – for reasons of preferring peace to the territories, since peace was seen as the best guarantee for security, or because of the "demographic problem" – the statistical gap between the natural population growth of the Palestinians and

Table 3.3. Bloc distribution in the Knesset, 1977–2006

Year	Right-wing bloc	Left-wing bloc	Center bloc
1977	63	42	15
1981	64	52	4
1984	61	53	6
1988	65	55	–
1992	59	61	–
1996	66	50	4
1999	60	48	12
2003	69	36	15
2006	50	34	36

Source: Knesset website www.knesset.gov.il.

that of Jewish Israelis, endangering the continued existence of a Jewish majority in Eretz Yisrael from the Mediterranean Sea to the Jordan River.

The reasoning behind each of the two stances was a force to be dealt with, and the public had difficulty deciding between them. The right wing tended toward the hawkish position; the left toward the dovish position; and the center usually tended toward the dovish position, with a few exceptions. Table 3.3 shows the bloc distribution resulting from the elections over the past three decades. The significance of the data is the lack of a clear mandate for solving the central problem on the political agenda. For almost thirty years the Knesset was split, with an extremely small alternating majority, and with a light tendency to the right for most Knesset terms.

Fragmentation and Sectorialism

Although the governmental system in Israel is parliamentary, voting is relative (one votes for a list of candidates presented by a party, with no dimension of personal election), and the level of representativeness is higher than is common in most Western countries. Those factors lead to an abundance of small parties, and thus each prime minister must spend a considerable amount of his time maintaining his coalition by dividing out political payoffs and spoils. The sectoral parties (such as the religious parties) are likely to support or even participate in a coalition whose policy on the central national issue is very different from theirs, as long as their constituents' real interests are well compensated:

for example, by considerable state budgetary funding for their separate education system. For the Ultra-Orthodox parties, such funding
is an existential interest, as it allows the existence of the society of
learners, exempt from military service and work, which has characterized Israel's Ultra-Orthodox society for the past three decades in
complete contradiction to what is common among Ultra-Orthodox
Jews in Europe and the United States.

In order to attain a parliamentary majority to approve his policies,
the prime minister has had to fulfill the demands of groups whose
nominal power is relatively small, but whose real power is great, as
they constitute the final vote for a winning coalition. Thus it was
in Likud governments, which despite their tendency to the right
enjoined the Ultra-Orthodox parties of moderate political orientation,
primarily in light of Likud's positive attitude toward religious tradition. Labor Party prime ministers used the same strategy. They needed
the support from within the right-wing camp, and by the spoils system – by granting political payoffs beyond a party's nominal strength,
or granting personal political payoffs for crossing party lines – they
succeeded in receiving the Knesset's approval for policies for which
it was doubtful that they would have a majority according to bloc
distribution.

The Rabin government (1992–5) established a coalition with the
support of the Shas party (an Ultra-Orthodox party of Sephardic Jews
identified, in most aspects, with the right wing), but, in order to
attain Knesset approval for the implementation of the agreement with
the Palestinians, political manipulation was needed, including creating
a split in one of the right-wing parties and granting ministerial and
vice-ministerial positions to Knesset members who crossed over to the
government. That was necessary since Shas members were unwilling
at that point to support the Oslo process, after their support of the
agreement at the first stage had led to sharp attacks on them and their
spiritual leader, Rabbi Ovadia Yosef, the religious figure with the most
influence among Mizrachim, who had served as the Sephardic Chief
Rabbi.

The political tie has led four times in the past three decades to
the establishment of governments shared by the two main parties: in
1984, 1988, 2001, and 2006. Cooperation has developed from the con-
straint stemming from the parliamentary balance of power, as shown
in Table 3.3. The result of the cooperation, however, was only a temporary reduction of the smaller parties' political power and temporary

stabilization. In the longer run the national unity governments blurred the ideological differences between the parties and increased the attractiveness of the smaller parties whose agenda remained coherent. Moreover, the coalition formations themselves have made the entire political system less reliable and led, on the one hand, to attempts for structural reforms and, on the other hand, to the search for alternative channels of political influence (see chapter 6).

The rotational national unity government established in 1984 survived the performance of the prime ministerial rotation in 1986, pursuant to the agreement. In the 1988 election the possibility of establishing a right-wing government arose, but the elected prime minister, Yitzhak Shamir, chose not to depend upon the radicals in the right-wing camp and preferred the framework of a national unity government, despite the fact that it hurt the chances of realizing the ideology of Greater Israel, in which he believed and in whose name he was elected. The government established in 1988 was a coalition government shared by Likud and Labor, yet without rotation. It lasted two years, until the outbreak of the political crisis which was called by then defense minister Yitzhak Rabin *haTargil haMasriach* ("the stinking trick").

The background to the crisis was the American administration's initiative to jumpstart the political process between Israel and the Palestinians, a process which had been paralyzed as a result of the Palestinian Intifada. The leader of the Labor Party was Shimon Peres, finance minister of the 1988 government, foreign minister from 1986 to 1988, prime minister from 1984 to 1986, and president of the State of Israel since 2007. Previously he had been defense minister in the Rabin government (1974–7), and had held various ministerial positions since serving in the 1950s in the role of director general of the Defense Ministry, as one of David Ben-Gurion's assistants. Peres saw in the American initiative, beyond its diplomatic value, an opportunity to alter the makeup of the coalition and to establish a government led by him. Peres counted on the support of religious parties. The Shas party was at that time of "dovish" orientation regarding the issue of "land for peace" despite its sociopolitical connection to the right-wing camp, and the Ultra-Orthodox 'Agudat Yisrael' party was bitter that the Shamir government had not honored promises made to it in coalition agreements.

In a no-confidence vote in the Knesset Shimon Peres voted against the government, and Prime Minister Shamir dismissed him immediately. As a result of his dismissal, all the ministers from the Labor

Party resigned, and the government fell. For two months Israel was in an acute political crisis: Peres nearly succeeded in establishing an alternative government, but at the last moment his religious partners, who preferred partnership with the right wing for ideological and theological reasons, backed out; and ultimately Shamir established a narrow right-wing government, which lasted until the elections in 1992. During the crisis there had been a number of crossings over by Likud Knesset members, accompanied by promises of personal advancement, a fact which caused rage and frustration within the party and in the public.

The public outrage over these political maneuvers led to the adoption of a number of constitutional amendments, which limited Knesset members' ability to leave the party in whose name they were elected and yet remain members of the Knesset or the government, and prohibited public sector employees from participating in the process of internal party elections. Most important, a new version of Basic Law: The Government was enacted[3] that changed the governmental system in Israel from a parliamentary one, similar to that of Great Britain (excepting the parliamentary election system), to a mixed form of parliamentary-presidential government: the voter votes with one ballot for the list of Knesset candidates he or she supports, and with another ballot for the prime ministerial candidate he or she supports. The prime minister, according to this law, would serve by force of direct election by the public, but the Knesset could bring a vote of no confidence, which would lead to a new general election. The makeup of the government – the names of the ministers and the division of portfolios between them – required Knesset approval: thus the basic law did not eliminate the need to establish a parliamentary coalition, as discussed below, in order to ensure the establishment of the government and its political survival.

The objective of the change was to prevent crises like *haTargil haMasriach* by stabilizing the governmental system via the direct election of the prime minister. However, de facto, another trend altogether developed. As shown in table 3.2, instead of the establishment of a

---

[3]   Israel has still not completed the process of establishing a constitution. According to a decision by the first Knesset, the constitution is established via the enactment of basic laws which are to become chapters of the state constitution. To date eleven basic laws have been passed, a few of which determine the basic values of the state, others of which arrange the activity of the branches of government. Basic Law: The Government was first enacted in 1969, was drafted anew in 1992, and then once again in 2001.

central ruling party and a few satellite parties as junior coalition partners opposed by a central opposition party with a few small opposition
parties, what occurred was a diffusion of the political system. There
were no more large parties, only medium-sized and small ones. The
reason for this was the opportunity that this unique electoral system
granted to every voter to vote for a prime minister according to his
or her stance regarding the central problem on the national agenda –
which was usually his or her stance regarding the Palestinian–Israeli
conflict – yet in voting for the Knesset, to choose the party close to
his heart in other respects. Thus the Shas party grew at the expense of
Likud, and the Labor Party shrank as the left wing and center grew.
As a result, the political weight of the prime minister's coalition partners grew, negatively affecting governmental stability. The basic law's
objectives had been frustrated, and its supporters claimed that the failure was a result of the compromises made in the process of legislating
it in the Knesset.

The direct election law was in effect for only five years: it was
legislated in 1992, but went into effect in 1996, lasting until 2001.
During those five years the citizens of Israel went to the ballot box to
elect a prime minister three times: in 1996 Benjamin Netanyahu was
elected, in 1999 Ehud Barak was elected, and in 2001 Ariel Sharon
was elected. The short terms of prime ministers made the proper management of the state's affairs difficult. The prime minister served by
force of direct election, but the government served by force of Knesset
approval. Thus there was still a need to establish coalitions of parties
who did not always see eye to eye on the problems of the state and
the ways to deal with them. Furthermore, the shrinking of the Likud
and the Labor Party, meant that there was no stable parliamentary ruling core for the legislation of statutes and for state budget funding
according to the policy of the government. Before every important
vote in the Knesset, bargaining took place between the prime minister or his representatives and his coalition partners. The political and
budgetary payoff needed to ensure the support of coalition partners
rose higher and higher, parallel to the waning of the strength of the
Likud and the Labor Party. And thus, instead of the stabilization of
the system and the prevention of the purchase of power by hand-
ing out benefits, the opposite situation was created: the government
was less stable, and even more dependent upon manipulations and
intrigues than it had been prior to the reform intended to prevent such
phenomena.

The direct election law caused agitation, and a lobby was established in the Knesset to revoke it, drawing political support from various circles. It was not only because of these considerations that Prime Minister Ariel Sharon decided to reinstate the previous governmental system, via a coalition of direct election opponents. The party whose interest was most harmed was the Likud. In the 1999 elections, the Likud fell to nineteen Knesset seats, whereas Shas, whose voters supported the Likud prime ministerial candidate (Netanyahu), grew to seventeen seats at Likud's expense. Although that electoral success should not be detached from the protest that encompassed many Mizrachim and Ultra-Orthodox against the judgment in the trial of Shas's political leader, Arye Der'i (the former interior minister who had been sentenced to three years in prison for taking a bribe), the common opinion in the Likud was that the direct elections law had granted the opportunity to vote for Shas, whereas otherwise many of its supporters would have continued to vote for Likud. And indeed, in the elections held after the revocation of the direct elections law (in 2003), Shas's strength diminished to eleven seats, and the Likud grew to thirty-eight seats, at the expense of all of its satellite parties.

The failed attempt at the direct election of the prime minister, accompanied by the dependency of the government itself upon the parliament, served to accentuate the chronic instability problem. Basic Law: The Government was enacted three times – in 1969, 1992, and 2001 – in addition to a series of amendments on certain points in that basic law.

"The Constitutional Revolution"

As mentioned in note 3 to this chapter, Israel has not yet finished the creation of its constitution, mainly because of internal disagreements and various schisms. The Knesset Constitution, Law and Justice Committee drafted a constitution shortly before the last elections, but as of 2006 it has been neither approved nor rejected by the Plenary. With the gradual approval of eleven Basic Laws already, Israel has, in the words of former Supreme Court President Aharon Barak, "a cripple constitution." Until 1992 these basic Laws were largely procedural rules of governance that had little significance for the political debates. In 1992 the Knesset adopted two basic laws whose constitutional significance was, as Barak put it, revolutionary: Basic Law: Human Dignity and Liberty, and Basic Law: Freedom of Occupation.

The two basic laws entrenched human rights which for the most part had already been recognized in Israeli law. Every person in Israel has a right to life, to liberty, to dignity, to his or her property, to privacy, to exit the country, and – if he or she is a citizen of the state – to enter it. The revolutionary significance of these basic laws was in the restriction of the authority of the legislative branch to violate those rights, and thus Israel turned from a parliamentary democracy in which parliament is omnipotent, to a de facto constitutional democracy in which parliament is restricted by the constitution. These basic laws determine that all branches of government must honor the rights safeguarded in them, and that duty naturally applies to the judicial branch as well. Thus, the Supreme Court held that these basic laws authorize it to examine whether the acts of the other branches of government are constitutional or not. That determination has far-reaching legal implications.

In Basic Law: Human Dignity and Liberty several important statements are made:

> "*Violation of Rights* (8). There shall be no violation of rights under this Basic Law except by a statute befitting the values of the State of Israel, enacted for proper purpose, and to an extent no greater than is required, or by regulation enacted by virtue of express authorization in such law."

The Knesset itself determined that restriction while acting as a constitutional convention, and it is thus not permitted, in its role as the legislative branch, to violate the human rights which it entrenched while acting as a constitutional convention. This is, in other words, the principle of constitutional supremacy over regular statutes. Violation of the rights safeguarded by the basic laws is unconstitutional, unless it is the product of the legislative process as defined in this three test article: fit with the values of the State of Israel, proper purpose, and proportionality. It is to be taken for granted that the decision whether a certain statute withstands the three tests is that of the court, which is authorized to invalidate the statute. The District or Magistrate Court can annul the statute for the purposes of the case before it, whereas the Supreme Court can annul it completely.[4]

---

[4]   That general ruling was made by the Supreme Court: CA 6821/93 *Bank Mizrachi Meuchad Ltd.* v. *Migdal, Cooperative Village*, 49 PD (4) 221 (1995). In a later judgment it was held

In practice, the Supreme Court exercises a self-restraint strategy, and from the time of the enactment of these basic laws (1992) until the end of 2006, it has annulled four statutes or statutory provisions. The first test in the process of judicial review of legislature is whether the statute fits the values of the state. "The values of the State of Israel" are defined in article one of the basic law (after its amendment in 1994) as follows:

> "*Basic Principles* (1). Fundamental rights in Israel are founded upon the recognition of the value of the human being, the sanctity of human life, and the principle that persons are free; these rights shall be upheld in the spirit of the principles set forth in the Declaration of the Establishment of the State of Israel.
> *Purpose* 1(a). The purpose of this Basic Law is to protect human dignity and liberty, in order to establish in a Basic Law the values of the State of Israel as a Jewish and democratic state."

This declaration opening the basic law has far-reaching significance. Human dignity, sanctity of human life, and human liberty are linked to the concept of a "Jewish and democratic state" stemming from the Declaration of the Establishment of the State of Israel of May 14, 1948. The courts had tended to interpret the laws of the state in accordance with the view of the state as the Jewish nation-state on the one hand, and as a democratic state on the other, but only in these basic laws is positive constitutional use made of this double concept. Moreover, these basic laws speak of "the values of the State of Israel as a Jewish and democratic state"; as constitutional language tends to do, this leaves the definition of the concrete values to statute and case law, assuming that a way can be found to harmonize and synchronize both systems of values: the Jewish, which includes national-Zionist components as well as religious-traditional components, and the democratic, whose values can of course be interpreted in different ways.

According to former President of the Supreme Court, Aharon Barak, in the event of a contradiction between the systems of values, the interpreter must raise the level of abstraction to the point at which the Jewish values and the democratic values converge. That position spurred controversy. Some say that instead of adopting the American model of judicial review entailing Supreme Court authority

that all basic laws, and not only those dealing with human rights, are of supra-statutory constitutional status: HCJ 3434/96 *Hoffnung* v. *The Chairman of the Knesset*, 50 PD (3) 57 (1996).

to invalidate laws which contradict the constitution, it would have been better to adopt the British model of declaring the existence of a contradiction between the constitution and its values, and the specific statute, and to remand final decision to the Knesset. On the other hand, the difference between the political cultures may question the adaptability of the British model. An additional argument that has been raised is that only the Supreme Court should be authorized to judicially review the constitutionality of statutes. Since the constitution has not been completed yet, it is safe to assume that Israel will continue the academic and political debate of these questions in the coming years.

The Court, the Parliament and the Public

The very discussion of the values arising from the language of the basic laws, and to an even greater extent the discussion of the concrete contents of those values, of the settlement of the contradictions, or of determining a hierarchy between them, is likely to be a matter of public controversy. The confidence of the public in the legal system is expressed in the fact that the legal decision of questions of fact, of interpretation of statutes, or of procedure, will enjoy consensus. Naturally, however, the legal decision of questions of values is likely to stray from the boundaries of consensus, if only since the rejected values-based stance is in many cases likely to be legitimate, or to be seen as legitimate by a considerable part of society. This is especially true in Israel, where ideological clashes between religious and secular, Arabs and Jews, or doves and hawks are translated into concrete political dilemmas. When the political system, as described above, is unable to provide answers to these dilemmas, they are often brought to the court (see also chapter 6). Even prior to the enactment of the basic laws and the considerations of values involved in interpreting them, the courts found themselves in the public arena, making decisions affecting the policy of the government. An example of that is the judgment of Supreme Court President Emeritus Moshe Landau ordering the government to refrain from establishing the settlement of Elon Moreh on the site that had been chosen, as that site would necessitate the expropriation of private Palestinian land for paving an access road.[5] That was a revolutionary judgment, which dealt a blow not only to the settlement policy of the government, but also to its abovementioned

---

[5]   HCJ 390/79 *Duikat v. The Government of Israel*, 31 PD (1) 1 (1979).

ideological infrastructure. As expected, the judgment sparked political controversy, but the government fulfilled the judgment, and Begin repeated what he had said when the High Court of Justice had ruled in a way which was comfortable for his government: "there are judges in Jerusalem."

Against the background of the governability distress, the power of the Supreme Court increased during the three decades under discussion. Not only do regular citizens turn to the Supreme Court sitting as the High Court of Justice with petitions against the government and the Knesset; politicians also petition the High Court of Justice against their colleagues, against the legislative branch, and against the executive branch. In recent decades the Supreme Court has been asked to decide questions such as establishing settlements in the occupied territories, dismantling of settlements established in the occupied territories, use of torture against terrorists in order to prevent acts of terrorism, the establishment of the security fence and its location, the authority of the prime minister to dismiss ministers who might disagree with his opinion, violation of the principle of equality regarding the duty of military service, suspension of certain human rights in light of the necessities stemming from the war on terrorism, and the like. Every judicial decision in petitions such as these, whether the decision allows or rejects the petition, means intervention in policymaking.

In light of the constitutional developments on the one hand, and the relative weakness of the other two branches of power on the other hand, Israel has joined a line of states in which a phenomenon which can be called "Juristocracy" has developed in recent decades. To a greater and greater extent, politics undergo legal transformation and are decided in legal proceedings in the judicial arena. This global trend is sharply felt in Israel, on the basis of the unique characteristics of the Israeli political system, which must choose between difficult and fateful decisions at a time when it is in a confidence crisis and a state of chronic instability. One of the manifestations of the crisis is the reliance upon judicial commissions of inquiry in cases of policy failure and performance failure, from the first Lebanon war (1982) to the second Lebanon war (2006), the collapse of bank stock-trading (1983), the assassination of Prime Minister Rabin (1995), and the relations between the state and the Arab minority (2000).

The purpose of these commissions is to bring about quasi-judicial decisions regarding the assignment of responsibility for the undesirable results, and to make recommendations regarding the organizational and operative lessons to be learned. The recommendations regarding specific persons bind the government, whereas the recommendations regarding the system are left to its discretion. That rule was determined as a result of the recommendation of the commission of inquiry headed by then Supreme Court President Yitzhak Kahan, to dismiss Defense Minister Ariel Sharon because of his indirect responsibility for the 1982 massacre in the Palestinian refugee camps in Beirut committed by units of the Christian phalanges in Lebanon. Thus the role of assigning responsibility was transferred from the government and the Knesset to a legal commission of inquiry, and the dismissal of a minister owing to functional or ethical failure became a punishment instead of a political result.

Toward a Turning Point

At the beginning of the twenty-first century a dramatic ideological development occurred, leading to immediate results on the political plane. Prime Minister Ariel Sharon decided to dismantle and destroy the Israeli settlements that had been established in the Gaza Strip, Palestinian territory which from 1948 to 1967 had been under Egyptian occupation and since 1967 under Israeli occupation. Sharon's decision caused a split in the Likud. The Gaza Strip had been a part of the territory of the British Mandate and, according to Likud ideology, that territory was supposed to become part of the State of Israel. During the peace negotiations with Egypt, Begin had unequivocally and totally rejected proposals – including those made by US President Jimmy Carter – to grant the Egyptians status in the Gaza Strip. Sharon himself had been in charge of establishing settlements in the occupied territories, and as far back as his military service in charge of IDF Southern Command had dealt with creating infrastructure for settlement in Gaza. After the Six Day War there had been an Israeli consensus that the Gaza Strip would be part of the State of Israel, in order to create a territorial buffer between Egypt and Israel. When it turned out that incorporating Gaza into Israel was not a practical possibility, for demographic reasons, the idea was raised that a bloc of Israeli settlements should be established in Gaza, thus creating the buffer between Israel and Egypt. Thus, both ideologically and strategically, Sharon's decision to dissolve the Israeli presence in the strip was a dramatic turning point.

The split of the Likud in 2005 was a natural result of that move. Revisionist Zionism had stood, since the days of Ze'ev Jabotinsky, for Greater Israel, and any deviance from that principle was considered heresy. It is no wonder that a considerable part of the Likud was unwilling to accept the turn in policy which the Sharon government had made. On the other hand, opinion polls were good to Sharon, and predicted that he would receive forty Knesset seats, or even more, if he left the Likud and established a party to compete in Knesset elections. Although the disengagement policy itself was approved, the government did not have a majority in the Knesset for some of the issues vital for its functioning, and the difficulties created by Gaza disengagement policy opponents ultimately led Sharon to the decision to establish a new party, called "Kadima."

A short time after the establishment of "Kadima" in early 2006, Sharon suffered a severe stroke, and has since been comatose. Ehud Olmert was chosen in his stead, and won the spring 2006 elections, albeit with a shrunken majority – twenty-six seats; requiring him to make far-reaching concessions in the coalition negotiations. Previously, during the election campaign, Olmert announced a program called *hitkansut* (convergence) – dismantling some of the settlements in the West Bank and concentrating them in the settlement bloc adjacent to Israel's sovereign territory, which would be formally annexed to Israel. According to the plan, if such a result would not be possible through negotiations with the Palestinians, Israel would execute it unilaterally. In presenting his government to the Knesset, Olmert even stated that its goal is to bring about the partition of Eretz Yisrael and the establishment of two states, the already existent Israel and a Palestinian state, and that the idea of partition will ensure the continued existence of Israel as a Jewish and democratic state. The weakening of security conditions in Israeli towns and villages close to the Gaza Strip, however, weakened the prospects of repeating the unilateral strategy in the West Bank.

Presenting partition as the rescue of the Zionist idea is a turning point in Israeli political discourse, and it affects the stance of the Likud as well. In autumn 2006 the Likud was split not over the very idea of partition or establishment of a Palestinian state, rather over the unilateral execution of the idea, outside the framework of an agreement. The Likud's position is that all is up for negotiation, and that there will be concessions in an agreement. Thus, incidentally, Sharon began his disengagement process from the ideology of Greater Israel. The issue is no longer an ideological rift, rather the evaluation of the situation: the weighing up of political and strategic factors. It is quite possible that Israel is about to reach a turning point, and recognize that its national interest requires separation from the Palestinians, even at the price of conceding a considerable part of the settlements which in the past seemed necessary for the national interest. Seeing as not everyone will be willing to concede "Greater Israel," it is to be assumed that there will be additional organizational developments in the right-wing camp. Those will obviously have implications for the capacity to govern. However, it is not clear at the moment whether they will reinforce the capacity to govern, or weaken it; if they will work to stabilize the governmental system, or do the opposite – actually further weaken stability because of the lack of a clear ideological path. Only after the internal Israeli territorial debate comes to an end will the political and governmental system be able to stabilize according to the new coordinates. From that point of view, the coming decade is likely to be captivating.

Further Reading

Barak, Aharon 2006. *A Judge in Democracy*. Princeton: Princeton University Press

Dowty, Alan 2005. *Israel/Palestine*. London: Polity

Hirschl, Ran 2004. *Towards Juristocracy: the Origins and Consequences of the New Constitutionalism*. Cambridge, MA: Harvard University Press

Naor, Arye 2005. "Hawks' beaks, doves' feathers: Likud prime ministers between ideology and reality," *Israel Studies* 10, 3, pp. 154–91

Peri, Yoram (ed.) 2000. *The Assassination of Yitzhak Rabin*. Stanford: Stanford University Press

4

Political Economy: Liberalization and Globalization

Guy Ben-Porat

Debates over the right economic order and the relation between politics and the economy have taken place since the early period of Zionism. The centrality of the "political" and the state-led economy in Israel (or the pre-state institutions) were challenged by demands for liberalization and for allowing private enterprise. In early statehood, however, while private capital played an important role, it was the state that dominated the economy. It was only in the 1980s that the market began to dis-embed from political control and the market economy became a dominant idea and political force. Thus, since the 1980s the Israeli economy has gone through a process of rapid liberalization, away from being state-led and towards becoming a Western-type liberal economy in lifestyle and division of labor, well integrated into the global economy and with growing gaps between rich and poor. These economic and social developments are related to and underscore many of the developments described in other chapters: the transformation of social cleavages, changes in the political system, land allocation, and the rise of "alternative politics."

After a slowdown in 2000 – a result of the "local" conflict and the global recession – the Israeli economy is showing growth but also problems of inequality and poverty. Israel's GDP per capita of above 19,000 (or 27,000, based on purchasing power parity) and a growth rate between 4 and 5 percent in the past five years brings it to the lower levels of the Organization for Economic Cooperation and Development (OECD) states. The contemporary Israeli economy has shifted from being based on agriculture, light industry, and labor-intensive production to a globalized knowledge-based economy with a growing high-tech sector of telecommunications, IT, and electronics. Lacking natural resources, Israel's economic growth depends on human

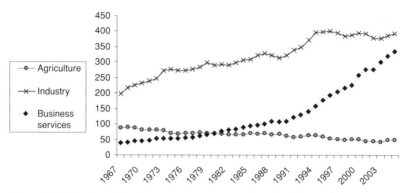

Figure 4.1. Number of employees per sector, 1967–2005 (in thousands)
Source: Bank of Israel. Retrieved from www.bankisrael.gov.il/series/catalog/labor%
20force,%20employment%20and%20wages/employed%20persons/

capital and, because of its small domestic market, it relies on trade
and exports. Israel's largest trade partners are the United States and
the European Union, which accounted in 2002, respectively, for 31
and 30 percent of exports and 22 and 40 percent of imports. Israel
established free trade agreements with its major partners, and is one of
the few countries in the world that holds free trade agreements with
both the United States and the European Union. While in the past
the Israeli economy was influenced by geopolitics and the conflict,
its globalization means that it is now also influenced by international
developments.

State-Led Economy

The Israeli state has been a major factor in economic development.
Prior to statehood, in the process of nation- and state-building, the
political institutions of the Zionist movement dominated the mobilization of capital, coming mainly from Jewish donations, and, consequently, the purchase of land and its development. This domination
enabled the Zionist movement to shield the Jewish workers from Arab
competition and to establish Jewish settlements based on the Zionist
collectivist ethos. This ethos underscored the commitment to nation-
and state-building that denounced individualism and private gain. This
collectivism, as several sociologists have noted, was less a (universal)

socialist ideology, in spite of the rhetoric of the founding fathers, than Jewish nationalism. Differently stated, unfavorable demography, lack of sovereignty, and limited resources led the Zionist movement to adopt collectivism as a method of nation- and state-building. The private sector was too small to have sufficient political influence to have an impact on the course of economic development and was overshadowed by the collectivist institutions of the Zionist movement. The labor federation, the Histadrut, formed in the pre-state period, evolved to become a significant economic and political player in the formative period of the state. The Histadrut was not only a Labor federation engaged in wage bargaining but also a provider of many social services, from education and culture to a sick fund and a bank. Moreover, the Histadrut was also a major employer in the different companies it owned. Like the Zionist movement, the Histadrut was dominated by the Labor Party and this dual control was at the base of the party's hegemony until 1977.

Independence in 1948 positioned the state, the inheritor of the Zionist institutions, in a dominant position over the economy. The state's dominance of the economic realm was a result of, on the one hand, the challenges of immigrant absorption, defense, and infrastructure building and, on the other hand, its control over the vast supply of incoming capital, from Jewish communities abroad and financial compensation from Germany on behalf of world Jewry after the Holocaust. To this one must add the Arab lands that passed into the hands of the government when the Arabs fled or were deported during the war. The state, as Michael Shalev explains, was positioned strategically, as the factor that directed immigration and settlement, the disposal of foreign gifts, and housing and industrial policy.[1] The result was a highly politicized and closely regulated economy with partially competing blocs of public, private, and Histadrut capital. Both the state and the Labor Party that dominated it had the capacity to steer business interests and civil society rather than be steered by them.

In economic terms the dominance of the state translated into high levels of government expenditure and employment relative to the economy's level of development, extensive state control of savings, investment and foreign currency, and modest public ownership, alongside a high degree of public subsidy of private and Histadrut-owned

---

[1]   Michael Shalev, "Liberalization and the transformation of the political economy." In G. Shafir and Y. Peled (eds.) *The New Israel: Peacemaking and Liberalization.* New York: Westview Press, 2000.

business. This high level of economic involvement was achieved not only by high taxes and resources drawn from abroad but also by appropriation of the bulk of household savings and control of their allocation to public and private investment. The relationship between the Histadrut and the Labor Party enabled the former to build a business empire that accounted for 25 percent of economic enterprises in Israel. As a trade union, it represented almost 80 percent of the workforce and, consequently, had significant power in wage negotiations with the government and employers.

Overall, the position of the state can be compared to other developmental states with a centralized economy. Through differential customs duties and other barriers to curtail imports the government protected local produce and import substitutes and encouraged export. Israel followed other newly industrializing countries in establishing a highly protective trade regime. Agriculture provides a good example of the relation between the state's economic intervention and the state's political goals. Agriculture was not only a means of production for many new settlements in the periphery (see chapter 2) but also a part of the Zionist national ethos of the New Hebrew Man and his attachment to the land through physical labor. The government's control over land, water, and credit was in itself a tool to direct agricultural production, but in addition it set up "marketing boards" to maintain the prices of agricultural produce. This was done either by the imposition of produce quotas (often blamed to be distributed according to political considerations or favoratism) or, in extreme cases, by destroying surplus. Much of this agriculture foundered in the 1980s when competitive measures were introduced and imports were allowed.

The roots of the Israeli welfare state can also be identified in the pre-state period, when different welfare institutions were developed. Residual and selective programs of social assistance to distressed and marginalized populations, which were implemented at the local level, and a comprehensive but exclusivist system of "mutual aid" were established by the Histadrut, providing its members with health services, pensions, unemployment relief, employment services, and housing. The construction of public housing by the state became one of the central domains in which the Israeli welfare state was active in the planning, design, financing, construction, and distribution of housing assets. As part of the "immigrant absorption" and "population dispersal" policies in early statehood (see chapter 2) resources were directed to supply houses for the mass immigration of the first years of statehood by subsidized housing and through state- and Histadrut-owned companies established to supply houses.

In the second decade after independence the welfare state institutionalized, formalized, and expanded to engage with social demands. These developments included national insurance and social assistance programs such as children's allowances, local welfare bureaus, and the improvement of social protection of vulnerable groups. These policies were expanded in the the early 1970s, when large social gaps between the veteran Ashkenazi and new immigrant population created social tensions. They included unemployment insurance, disability insurance, and a guaranteed minimum income. By 1977 the welfare system had expanded greatly to cover most of the population against loss of income, redistributed incomes to narrow income differentials, and reduced the incidence of poverty.

Crisis and Liberalization

The state continued to play a pivotal role in the economy in the following decades. After a recession in the mid-1960s and the war of 1967 came the "military-industrial complex" based on government-subsidized local military procurement, growing demand for arms, and the US government's financing of Israel's foreign arms purchases. In the middle of the 1980s the structure of the Israeli economy was close to that of most developed nations, with agriculture accounting for about 5 percent of the GNP, industry for 30 percent, and services for 65 percent. By 2006 the figures were: agriculture 2.6 percent, industry 30.8 percent, and services 66.6 percent.

Like many of the developed economies, Israel suffered the implications of the recession of the 1970s, with lower growth rates. The economic downturn was exacerbated by Israel's regional and internal difficulties and its high defense expenditures. An economic crisis evolved in the 1970s, which included an increasing deficit in the external balance of payments and an increasing inflation. The state, despite subsidizing and protecting large businesses, was unable to control them owing to internal political difficulties, and, with growing demands, the deficits of the public sector soared. Excessive deficit spending, frequent recourse to corrective devaluations, and government lending policies led to economic stagnation and inflation that reached its peak in the middle of the 1980s.

The election of the Likud in 1977, after twenty-nine years of Labor dominance, has not led to a significant change in economic policy, despite Likud's support of free-market economics, and the deficits have continued to grow. The period between 1974 and 1985 is described by economists as Israel's "lost years." Inflation spiraled in this period (reaching a monthly rate of 10 to 25 percent in 1984), tax receipts fell drastically and increased the budget deficit (average of 12 percent of GNP between 1980 and 1984). Fears that the government would fail to honor its liabilities caused an outflow of capital abroad, and stock market speculation and government inattention produced an unprecedented crisis in the banking system. By 1985 the economic crises came to pose a real threat to the state's fundamental legitimacy and to its economic viability. The national unity government, formed in 1984 after a tie in the elections and the looming crisis, faced a severe challenge. Inflation reached 444 percent in 1984, a huge foreign debt reached 80 percent of GNP, foreign currency reserves were decimated, the trade balance was in high deficit, a huge public sector debt (internal and external) reached 250 percent of GNP, and the economy suffered a slowdown after a stock market crisis in 1983.

The emergency Economic Stability Plan initiated by the national unity government in 1985 headed by Shimon Peres not only brought the economy back from the brink of hyperinflation but also inaugurated a structural shift of liberalizing Israel's political-economic regime. Internally, the work of a group of professional economists, trained in the Chicago school tradition, played an important role in the planning and execution of the reforms. Externally, the pressure of the United States government was also significant, as it tied its $1.3 billion to the Israeli government commitment for reforms and to a detailed plan written jointly by Israeli and American economists. The government's stabilization program included a balancing of the budget by drastic cuts in subsidies, cuts in aid to factories, dismissal of employees, gradual reduction in domestic defense spending, and an increase of the real interest rate. The government also devalued the shekel (local currency) and then stabilized the nominal rate of exchange and made a real wage cut through a reform of the wage indexation system. These measures led to a dramatic reduction in inflation and in the public sector's budgetary deficit. Productivity began to increase, exports surged, imports shrank, and confidence in the shekel gradually returned. The economic plan not only managed to curb the spiraling inflation but also transformed the Israeli economic structure away from its protectionist and state-centered formation into a more neo-liberal type of economy. In Israel as elsewhere, the process of economic liberalization meant the contraction of the state and a larger role for markets in economic management, namely, privatization, government expenditure reduction, tax cuts, and deregulation. Since the late 1980s Israel's capital market has gone through various reforms intended to integrate it into global capital markets. These have included an automated trading system and a paperless clearinghouse linked since 2002 with the American Depository Trust Company (DTC) to simplify cross-border settlement for shares of dually listed companies. In 1993 the derivatives market was opened, which facilitated risk management for individual and institutional investors with a growing number of products.

By the end of the 1980s, in spite of the economic changes, the state was still the owner of most of the land, energy resources, radio and television, defense industries, and airline transportation. Some 200 state-owned companies remained intact, including monopolies such as the telephone company. The public sector remained large, with almost 30 percent of employed persons working for the government. The holding company of the Histadrut still accounted for almost 15 percent of the GNP in 1991. Plans for privatization of government- and Histadrut-owned companies were supported by the IMF and the liberal economists in the Israel Ministry of Finance but were at most partially implemented because, first, the Histadrut held enough power at that stage to curb these attempts and, second, many of the companies had substantial debts that made privatization difficult. The liberalization of the Israeli economy was also held back by political developments, as the outbreak of the Palestinian uprising in 1987 (see chapter 1) increased the costs of occupation and curbed Israel's globalization.

The economic plan had several important implications for the Israeli economy and society that unfolded in the 1990s. The significance of the economic plan beyond its successful reduction of inflation was in recasting the Israeli economic structure away from its protectionist and state-centered formation into a more neoliberal type of economy. The Histadrut, whose enterprises were heavily in debt, was concerned with its affiliated pension funds and health service and had limited power to resist the plan and, in the following years, lost more of its ability to curb the liberalizing agenda. The economic plan and the weakness of the Histadrut also enabled the privatization of government-owned companies. In 1985 there were about 160 companies and the number was reduced to less than 100 by 2002. These privatizations were designed to encourage competition and improve services but also as a means for financing budget deficits.

Also important was the development of an autonomous business community, which, as will be discussed later, had the desire and a growing ability to integrate globally. With the liberalization of the capital market the private sector was able, for the first time, to raise capital through the stock exchange, free from government control. Moreover, Israeli corporations began floating their securities on the New York Stock Exchange. Exposure to competition from import substitutes increased after the stabilization plan, as Israel gradually began to honor its free trade agreements with the European Union (1975) and the United States (1985). The increasing competition and the massive cuts in subsidies that hurt business were offset by tax cuts of a similar magnitude. Revenues from corporate income and payroll taxes rose sharply relative to national product immediately after stabilization, but tax rates and subsidies were then reduced by reforms.

Beyond the concrete economic impact of the reforms, an ideational change took off that provided the legitimacy for the further development of neoliberalism. An economic logic based on profit and efficiency, advocating privatization, deregulation, and competition became paradigmatic, against the centralized welfare state conception. By the 1990s the Israeli economy was both liberalized, in terms of a shift to market economics, and in the course of becoming globalized, integrated in the world economy. With the shrinking of state control over capitalist markets, the decline of the Histadrut, the reduction of monopolies, and the convergence of the two main parties towards a neoliberal economic agenda, Israel's economic policies resembled those of many other Western states. In practice, however, after the 1980s capital was concentrated again, but in the hands of private owners who began to dominate the Israeli economy. It was in the 1990s that the economic developments described above began to unfold because of three main factors: the wave of immigration from the former Soviet Union (FSU), the high-tech boom, and the peace process.

The 1990s – Immigration, Peace, and Globalization

In the 1990s the pace of the developments described above picked up so that Israel achieved a wave of growth comparable with the Asian

Tigers, living standards with the reach of the OECD democracies and a globalization that ranked it in 1996 at 18 out of 46 countries – including all of the OECD and the rapidly growing newly industrialized countries (NICs) – by the *World Competitiveness Yearbook*. The economic take-off of the 1990s can be explained by three factors: the mass immigration of Jews from the FSU, the peace process with the Palestinians (see p. 16), and the high-tech industry that was part and parcel of a worldwide expansion. These factors in themselves, as Michael Shalev argues,[2] imply that in spite of liberalization the state still played a major role in economic development through its immigration and absorption policy (see chapter 2), foreign policy (see chapter 1), and educational investments. The state, however, while still a powerful entity, operates under different conditions and with a changed set of policies, consistently neoliberal.

The break-up of the Soviet Union in the late 1980s led to a mass immigration of Jews to Israel. Between 1990 and 1997 about 710,000 Russian Jews immigrated to Israel, increasing its working age population by 15 percent. This mass migration initially caused unemployment and lowered wages but in a relatively short time increased demand and investments. The fact that this immigration was on average highly skilled enabled its economic integration, so, after two years of high unemployment, by 1992 the immigrants' labor participation rates were equal to that of Israelis. The high skills of many of the immigrants also enabled them to take part in the high-tech boom in the 1990s. The quick absorption of the immigrants in the economy and the negative pressure that immigration exerted on wages led to an expansion in aggregate supply that was reflected in a high growth rate. From 1992 onwards the peace process became the dominant factor determining investment, as it encouraged local and foreign investments in the israeli economy and opened new markets for Israeli companies abroad.

The 1990s, therefore, were a decade of rapid growth as, after a long period of slow growth, overall economic growth measured in GDP reached 6.8 percent in 1994 and 7.1 percent in 1995. GDP per capita grew from $12,610 in 1992 to over $16,000 by the end of the decade. The Israeli economy became attractive for investors: in the early 1990s foreign direct investment averaged $240 million annually and by the last four years of the decade it averaged $2.4 billion, a tenfold increase. Israel's international risk rating markedly improved:

---

[2]   Ibid.

Euromoney ranked Israel in fifteenth place among states surveyed in the early 1990s and in twenty-ninth place by the end of the decade. Credit rating agencies such as Standard & Poor's and Moody's rated Israel, respectively, AA- and A2, interpreted as "high quality" and "strong payment capacity." Israel's economic growth, its fiscal policy, and the peace process were the explanations for the favorable rating. Beside the booming high-tech industry, the tourism industry – most sensitive to geopolitical developments – doubled itself, from an average of 1.4 million to 2.5 million visits, and the total revenue grew from $1.8 billion to $3.5 billion.

Liberalization and globalization, however, were accompanied by growing social disparities in Israel. Israel experienced considerable growth but the fruits of the 1985–95 cycle of prosperity have been unevenly distributed. The obvious winners are capitalists, business executives, and middlemen and women of the "professional," "service," or "new" class; the losers are unskilled laborers whose jobs were cut as a result of imports or relocation of the production process elsewhere. Like other countries, Israel in the process of globalization was moving away from being a welfare state to becoming a "competition state."

Peace, Globalization, and Economic Growth

The business community and politicians on the left of the political spectrum (see chapter 1) began in the late 1980s to make the connection between economic growth and peace. This was best captured by Shimon Peres's vision of a New Middle East (hereafter, NME) written in 1991, shortly before the Oslo Agreements. The NME was intended to provide a blueprint for the future of the region, based on economic rationality, peace, democracy, cooperation, mutual gain, and general prosperity. The choice the Middle East must face, Peres argued, is between peace, global integration, and progress or continuing conflicts and backwardness.

> Peace between Israel and the Arab states and the Palestinians will eliminate an important source of tension, if not the most dangerous. Instead of visions of blood and tears there will rise visions of happiness and beauty, life and peace. We are at a historic crossroads. Do we choose the path of the tongues of fire, billowing smoke, and

rivers of blood, or of blooming deserts, restored wastelands, progress, growth, justice and freedom? The higher the standard of living rises, the lower the level of violence will fall.

The linkage between peace and prosperity was also explicit in the 1992 election campaign platform of Meretz, the pro-peace liberal party:

> Peace agreement with our neighbors and a policy consistent with the values and interests of the democratic world will enable Israel to integrate into the world economy and into a stronger and expanding European Community, to become the recipient of investments and credit and to possess a progressive and exporting economy.[3]

Israeli businessmen developed high expectations from the Labor Party led by Yitzhak Rabin (Peres being a senior member), who in more practical and mundane language committed himself to compromise. Two days before the elections of 1992, when the polls indicated that the Labor Party would win, an improved business mood was reflected in the stock prices, which climbed by 3.5 percent, and after the elections results confirmed the expectations by another 7 percent. "Whereas in the ballot box investors vary in their political views," explained one economic analyst, "in the stock market there was largely a consensus. For most investors the return of the left (the Labor) means higher chances for conflict resolution."[4]

Four major factors were accounted for Israel's forecasted economic leap. First, the end of the Arab boycott would open markets for Israel in central Asia and the Far East. Second, multinational corporations, which hitherto had been reluctant to invest in Israel, would take advantage of the new opportunities that the peace process created. Third, direct trade between Israel and the Arab world would be established. And fourth, provided that genuine peace prevails, military expenditures could be reduced.

The economic developments that followed the signing of the Oslo Accords seem to confirm many of the optimistic scenarios and at least the first two factors described above. The stock market reflected the explosion of business optimism resulting from what one paper described as "investors betting on peace,"[5] reaching an unprecedented

---

[3]   Both quoted in Gershon Shafir, "Business in politics: globalization and the search for peace in South Africa and Israel/Palestine," *Israel Affairs* 5, 2 (1998), pp. 102–19.

[4]   Guy Rolnik, "Gaza and Jericho, but the National Bank first," *Haaretz* October 6, 1993.

[5]   See Guy Ben-Porat, *Global Liberalism, Local Populism: Globalization, Peace and Resistance in Israel/Palestine and Northern Ireland*, Syracuse, NY: Syracuse University Press, 2006, p. 172.

peak, breaking all records, three days after the signing. The papers drew a new map of the world with countries such as Tunisia, Malaysia, Cambodia, and Oman opening up to Israel and showing projected potential economic and political gains that Israel would experience. Israel was globalizing, as international credit rating agencies and multinational companies expressed growing confidence in Israel. The International Country Risk Guide (ICRG) improved Israel's rating from seventy-ninth out of 130 countries in 1991 to forty-third in August 1994. Merrill Lynch predicted in 1994 that Israel was expected to post high growth rates and the IMF in the spring of 1994 stated that "Israel presently enjoys the basic preconditions for high and sustainable medium-term economic growth."

The list of foreign companies that entered the Israeli market included, among others, major American retail chains such as Pepsi Cola, McDonalds, Burger King, Tower Records, Office Depot, and Ace Hardware. European, East Asian, and other companies also began operating in Israel. Daimler Benz opened a representative office in 1994, Heineken commissioned a plant to manufacture and distribute Amstel beer in Israel, Hyundai began marketing its cars, and Taiwan-based Acer decided to begin manufacturing in Israel. Its president explained that "When the peace process advances, we will upgrade our Israeli assembly plant to become the distribution center for neighboring states." Other companies bought shares in Israeli companies: Cable and Wireless purchased shares in Bezeq, the Israeli telephone company, Swiss giant Nestlé bought 10 percent of Osem, the second largest food company, and Canada's Northern Telecom purchased 20 percent of Telrad, an electronics company.

The High-Tech Economy

The structural changes that the Israeli economy has undergone in the 1990s have transformed it from a traditional economy to a high-tech and knowledge-based economy. The economic changes caused the shift of weight from the labor-intensive industries to the high-tech sector and, accordingly, a demand for high-skilled workers and a reduced demand for low-skilled workers. Israel's major exports became manufactured goods and software, which accounted for 97 percent of total exports (excluding diamonds, ships, and aircraft) in 2002. Agricultural exports accounted for 3 percent in 2000, compared to 16.5 percent in 1970, illustrating the depth of Israel's structural changes. The exposure to foreign competition and free trade agreements with countries with low-labor costs flooded the market with cheaper products and, consequently, decimated the traditional labor-intensive industries, such as textiles. Thus, between 1994 and 2003 employment in the textile and garment industries was almost halved. Conversely, in the same years employment in the high-tech or the information and communication technologies (ICT) almost tripled. This is matched by the rise of the education level in general and the higher number of engineers and technicians who answered to the growing demand of the industry. The educated workforce was also strengthened by the immigration from the former Soviet Union, which included a relatively high number of immigrants with engineering degrees. Another source of high-tech expertise was the Israeli defense force, as veterans of technological units found their way to the private sector.

A study of the Central Bureau of Statistics in 2002 found that high-tech employment accounted for 8 percent of total employment. The value of the high-tech industry, however, is not only in its size but in the overall impact on Israeli society and economy. The high-tech industry is significant to Israel's globalization described above, as thousands of companies of different sizes and a wide range of fields – mainly Internet, communications and software – have emerged in the last decade, some with notable global success. The high-tech companies have attracted the bulk of foreign investments since the 1990s, with a record high of $3.7 billion in 1999. Currently there are around a hundred Israeli companies trading in the US NASDAQ (National Association of Securities Dealers Automated Quotations) market and since 1995 about 150 high-tech companies have been purchased by international companies for a total sum of about $25 billion. Venture capital industry has also developed, using capital from global financial investors and multinationals to invest in local high-tech companies.

No less important is the cultural impact of high-tech, with the rise of young and successful entrepreneurs, some of whom have accumulated wealth on levels previously achieved only by inheritance, and introduced a new lifestyle and culture. One economic columnist described this as a different country emerging within Israel.

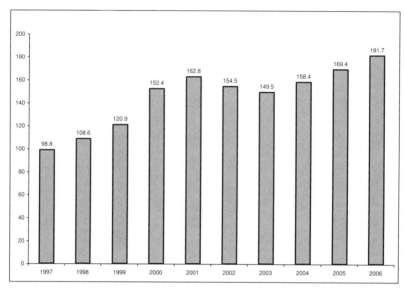

Figure 4.2. Number of employees in ICT industries in Israel, 1997–2006 (in thousands)
Source: Israel Central Bureau of Statistics, Press Announcement, May 14, 2007. Retrieved from www.cbs.gov.il

Take all the values upon which the Israeli economy was built: the collective, institutions, social security, political support – turn them over and you get the new high-tech industry's values. Risk taking is fashionable, individual entrepreneurship is most valued, detachment from every Israeli character and obedience to market forces, usually the American, is necessary. The high-tech industry is the "mixing" of the Israeli market: it is done by Israelis, in Israel, but it obeys, lives and breathes only the Western "religion" – the forces of Western market economy.[6]

A Consumer Society

Related to the developments described above are significant changes in patterns of consumption and culture described by some scholars as an "Americanization" of Israeli society. This transformation has included the introduction of consumerist behavior and values, leisure

[6] Guy Rolnik, "A different country," *Haaretz – a Hundred in Economy*, Special Supplement December 12, 1999.

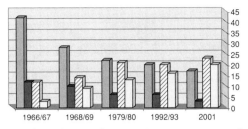

Figure 4.3. Monthly household expenditure for specific categories as a percentage of the total expenditure, 1967–2001
Source: Israel Central Bureau of Statistics, Household Expenditure Survey, *Statistikal* No. 29, December 2002. Retrieved from www.cbs.gov.il

activities and entertainment patterns and lifestyles into a previously relatively closed Israeli society with an ethos of collectivism. Thus, from a society of austerity in the 1950s, Israel has been turning into an affluent society, with more "hedonistic" values, open to foreign cultural influences, deeply engaged in consumption, and with a new ethos of individualism. Israelis, in other words, have become more and more concerned with the "good life." With the liberalization of trade described above, Israeli consumers are being offered a growing variety of products at lower prices, accelerated by electronic commerce and media advertising (see Figure 4.3).

Since the 1990s Israeli society has rapidly become part of the global economy and culture. American fast food and retail chains have been established across Israel, a new language imbued with English words and slang has been introduced, as well as rock music and other (mostly) American musical influences and a multi-channeled commercial television. The affluence, openness to foreign cultural influences, "hedonistic" values, and consumerism have been attested by the increase in the number of motor vehicles, electric appliances, and, later, mobile phones and Internet access (see Figure 4.4). During the 1990s many sorts of outdoor shopping malls sprang up throughout Israel. Entrepreneurs and urban planners tend to give names like "BIG" and "Mega" to these sites and generally refer to them as "power centers" since they represent large national and international businesses and big money. Blind to the constraints of religiosity, ethnicity, or family connections, these shopping centers speak to modernity and link Israelis of all sorts to the wide, Western, and mainly American world of plenty.

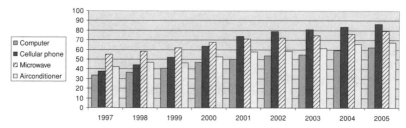

Figure 4.4. Ownership of consumer products per percentage of population, 1997–2005
Source: Israel Central Bureau of Statistics, Household Expenditure Survey 2006

Uri Ram outlines some of these developments of the "consumer revolution" that has taken place.[7] Private consumption in 1996 was 5.5 times higher than in 1950 and this rise is explained in spending on housing and various services, including foreign travel. The introduction of commercial television in the 1990s has turned watching television into the largest component of leisure time. Until the early 1990s Israel had only one television channel, operated by the government. Since then two new commercial channels and cable television have begun operating, bringing to viewers shows from all over the world, but mostly American productions. Consequently, the total spending on advertisement has risen to about $963 million in 1997. The number of motor vehicles quadrupled between 1966 and 1996. Israel is rated high in the world in numbers per capita of video cassette recorders (and, now, DVDs), personal computers, Internet connections, and mobile phones.

Mass Communication

The changes in communication since the 1980s provide a powerful demonstration of the social, economic, and cultural changes described throughout this book, and their relation to political changes. Whereas in 1980 Israelis had a one-channel TV controlled by the government, twenty-five years later they enjoy literally hundreds of channels from across the world, which cater to different desires and tastes. In addition, the Internet is a source of information and entertainment that

---

[7]   Uri Ram, "The promised land of business opportunities: liberal post-Zionism in the global age." In G. Shafir and Y. Peled (eds.) *The New Israel: Peacemaking and Liberalization.* New York: Westview Press, 2000.

provides more choices and opportunities. The process, therefore, is a shift from a non-liberal model of state control to a market-oriented media that caters to popular tastes and carves out specific cultural niches.

State monopoly of the media (radio and television) and the presence of newspapers associated with political parties alongside privately owned newspapers were characteristic of Israel's early statehood. The state's control over the newspapers, some privatized or run by opposition parties, was by censorship or through the "Editor's Committee," which was formed in the early years of statehood and brought together the editors of the central newspapers (excluding non-Zionist ones) for briefings with top government officials or bureaucrats on national security matters. These informative briefings were in fact a censorship exercise in which editors agreed to limit the publication of sensitive matters, including security issues.

The changes that occurred in the 1990s reflect other, wider changes in Israeli society and the development of a consumer society with a variety of tastes and demands. These demands were first met by semi-legal or illegal means, when pirate radio stations and illegal closed-circuit cable television channels became popular either for niche markets or for general demand.

In the middle of the 1980s the state moved in to regulate the means of communication and to provide legally what was hitherto provided by other means. The changes included franchises for operating cables, the establishment of eleven regional radio stations, two special-interest stations (Arab and Jewish-Orthodox), and a second television channel based on advertising revenues with relative political autonomy. These changes made illegal cable networks obsolete, but pirate radio stations continue to operate in spite of attempts to shut them down, especially as their broadcasts interfere on the airwaves with important services.

By the end of the 1990s mass communication had radically changed. In the print media the party newspapers have largely disappeared and one newspaper (*Yediot Aharonot*) dominates that market against its competitors, *Maariv*, *Haaretz* (which caters to the more educated), and *Globes* (a business newspaper). In addition there are newspapers aimed at different sectors (Arab, Religious, and Russian) and a growing variety of chromo magazines that capture different niches, such as sport and lifestyle. In Israel, as elsewhere, print media lags behind the electronic media. Television is divided between three "open" channels – the struggling state-owned television, the dominant commercial channel 2, and the relatively new commercial channel 10 – and subscription cable or satellite television, which offer a variety of channels and programs from the across the world. The Internet has also profoundly changed mass communication in Israel, with numerous websites, blogs, and chats that supplement or replace the more traditional media and offer new opportunities for expression and initiatives that are largely beyond the control of the state.

The transformation of the media is part of the general changes of Israel described in this book and more specifically of the economic changes described in this chapter. The politically controlled media (by state and political parties) have been replaced by an economic market-oriented media that are concentrated largely in the hands of a few business groups. This has led, on the one hand, to a more politically independent and critical media but, on the other hand, to new dependencies and limitations. The market approach means that the media are now part of the evolving consumer society, geared to advertisements and ratings and, consequently, appealing to a low common denominator that consumes "info-tainment" (information as entertainment).

The New Labor Force

The rate of participation in the labor force in Israel is low compared to other developed economies. The overall rate of participation in the civilian labor force for women in 2001 was about 48.4 percent and 60.7 percent for men. In two segments of the Israeli society, the Arab sector and the Ultra-Orthodox sector, the rate of participation in the labor force is particularly low, especially for women. While the Arab difficulties in the labor market are related to discrimination and limited opportunities, for the Ultra-Orthodox the avoidance of the labor market is often a result of the choice to study the Torah and live on government subsidies.

The global economy has also brought a change in the labor force. Not only has the distribution of occupation shifted (see p. 92) but deeper changes in the organization and characteristics of the labor force have taken place. Outsourcing, subcontracting, and privatization have weakened the bargaining power of workers. In the past about

80 percent of workers were unionized, whereas less than 40 percent belonged to unions in 2000. In many work places collective bargaining has been replaced by individual contracts or even, in many government ministries and agencies, work has been subcontracted to reduce costs and at times broken down to part-time jobs paid by the hour and devoid of fringe benefits. According to the findings of ADVA (a left-leaning, non-partisan, action-oriented Israeli policy analysis center), some 19 percent of part-time workers in 1999 reported that they wanted to work full time and in 2005 the figure had risen to 28.5.[8]

The composition of the labor force has also changed with the entry of foreign workers to Israel. The 1967 war provided Israel with a supply of cheap labor from the West Bank and Gaza for manual jobs. The decision to allow Palestinians to work in Israel was part of the effort to establish control over the newly occupied territories (see chapters 1 and 5) and also a response to economic demand for cheap labor. By the middle of the 1980s about 110,000 Palestinians were employed in Israel, mostly in construction, agriculture, and services. About one-third of the workforce in the West Bank and half of that of Gaza worked in Israel and constituted 6–7 percent of the Israeli workforce. These workers were not unionized and were deprived of many benefits enjoyed by Israeli workers.

Foreign workers with permits began to enter Israel in the 1980s, mostly in specific niches such as tourism and geriatric care, followed by workers in agriculture from Thailand. In the early 1990s, the rise in the demand for housing, on the one hand, and closures imposed on the territories on the other hand, led to the import of construction workers from Eastern Europe. In March 1993, after a campaign of Palestinian terror attacks, Israel imposed a series of closures on the territories, which prevented the entry of workers for a long period. Under pressure from constructors and farmers, the government opened the gates so that Israeli industrialists, farmers, and developers, with the government's permission, replaced Palestinian laborers with foreign laborers. Again, as in 1967, this development combined economic and political goals. The replacement of Palestinian workers was seen as a step in the separation of Israel from the West Bank and Gaza. In numbers, the change was dramatic, as in 1987 the government issued 2500 permits for foreign workers and by 1996 the number reached 130,000, with

---

[8]   The ADVA Research Center's reports are available at www.adva.org.il.

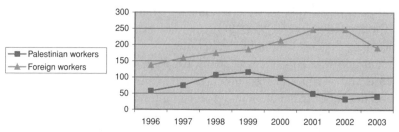

Figure 4.5. Palestinian and foreign workers – economic trends in Israel, 1996–2003
Source: Economics and Research Department, Israel Finance Ministry, December 2005, www.mof.gov.il

an unknown number of illegal workers. In response to the growing number of foreign workers (which, according to government figures, surpassed 200,000 in 2002) and the rise of unemployment in Israel, an Immigration Administration was formed in 2002 to prevent the entry and presence of illegal workers in Israel. Accordingly, the numbers of foreign workers was significantly reduced and the number of Palestinian workers has not risen (see Figure 4.5).

Rich and Poor

The globalization and liberalization of the Israeli economy have turned Israel not only into a consumer society but also into a highly unequal society with growing levels of poverty. Poverty rates in Israel fluctuated from a low of 12.8 percent in 1989 to a high of 18 percent in 1994, leveling at an average of about 16 percent in 1997. Several factors described above contributed to an increase in poverty and income inequality in Israel during the early 1990s: the mass migration that contributed to a rise in unemployment and underemployment, the expansion of the hi-tech industries contributed to an increase in the overall level of wage inequality, and unskilled and low income jobs were filled by guest workers, contributing to the rise of unemployment among the low-skilled population. To this one can add the lack of real competition in many of the economic branches, which brings excessive profits to the owners at the expense of the consumers, uneven growth between center and periphery, and the lack of a national comprehensive pension plan that causes high rates of poverty among the elderly. The decade of the 1990s, therefore, was a decade of growth unevenly distributed.

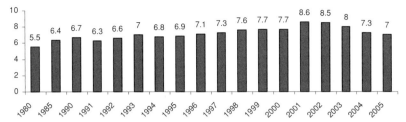

Figure 4.6. National expenditure for transfer payments relative to GNP, 1980–2005 (in percentages)
Source: Israel Finance Ministry. Retrieved from: www.mof.gov.il/budget2006/ index06.htm

The reports of the ADVA research center, based on data provided by the National Insurance Institute, provide a picture of the growing gaps and poverty. The income of the highest income decile has risen in tandem with the GDP but the income of the middle and lower deciles has hardly changed. The gap between the deciles, has accordingly widened. In 1990, measured in household incomes, the income of the top decile was 8.9 times that of the bottom decile; by 1999 it was 11.9 times higher. Similarly, while most salaried Israelis earn less than the average wage and less than their European counterparts, Israeli senior managers and officials earn salaries that are on par with those in Europe. The average monthly salary in Israel in 1998 was the equivalent of $1500, but high-ranking officials in the public sector earned five-digit salaries and in the private sector salaries were considerably higher. Thus, in 1994 senior managers earned thirteen times the average wage and by 1998 nineteen times the average wage. In 1999 72 percent of all Israelis earned the average wage or less and 63 percent earned less than 75 percent of the average wage.

The liberalization of the economy went hand in hand with the retrenchment of the welfare state and its universal services established in previous years. While the transfer payments (which grew in the 1990s see figure 4.6) were able to reduce poverty, the gaps between rich and poor and the levels of poverty remained higher in the 1990s than in the previous decade. Not only was the welfare state no longer able to prevent poverty effectively and criticized from the left, it was also criticized from the right by powerful voices that advocated greater liberalization. The universal services provided by the welfare state were gradually replaced by political ("clientalistic") services (especially religious), by third-sector organizations or by private and at times semi-legal means (see chapter 5). While the National Health Law of 1994 provided a universal package of medical services to all citizens, the cutbacks in health provisions (or the refusal to expand them to new medicines and treatments) have led to the development of a wide variety of supplemental private insurance plans. Similarly, in pension plans and education the provision of the state services was supplemented by private means (see chapter 5), which contributed to the growing gaps between rich and poor.

The rich in Israel have grown not only richer but also more politically powerful; the media has pointed again and again in recent years to the relations – social, political, and economic – between capital and government. In 2006 some eighteen Israeli families were found by a BDI (Business Data Israel) survey to control 32 percent of the revenues of the leading 500 companies in Israel and to employ some 150,000 workers.[9] The privatization of government-owned companies only contributed to the concentration of the economy as many of their shares were purchased by the same families. In 2006 the Israel Antitrust Authority expressed concern over these developments and promised to monitor carefully any merger relating to companies owned by these families.

Crisis and (More) Liberalization

At the end of the 1990s GDP per capita reached $17,900 and the economy was showing growth again after a slowdown between 1997 and 1999. But, the contraction of the economy in the following year indicated that Israel was experiencing a recession. The downturn demonstrated both Israel's globalization and the important impact of local/regional politics on the economy. Specifically, the economic crisis was a result of the global downturn in the high-tech sector and the collapse of the peace process in September 2000. The recovery of the economy three years later showed the same mixed blessing of the 1990s: economic growth and widening gaps and poverty.

Benjamin Netanyahu's almost accidental nomination as Minister of Finance in 2003, a result of a reshuffle tactic of Prime Minister Sharon

---

[9]   This survey can be found at www.bdi.co.il/EngDefault.aspx.

that moved him from the Ministry of Foreign Affairs, turned out to be a major development of neoconservatism in Israel. The Ministry of Finance allowed Netanyahu to maintain his hawkish hard-line foreign policy attitude but, more important, to concentrate on an ambitious economic plan that would gain support from significant constituencies. Especially important was the backing of the business community and the upper classes, traditionally supporters of the politically moderate Labor Party, who, during the political deadlock with the Palestinians, were ready to support Netanyahu, who promised to take on the welfare state and to further liberalize the economy. The policy Netanyahu advocated included budget cuts, privatization of government-owned companies, decreasing the public sector, and forcing people to move from welfare to work. Thus, the remains of the welfare state and unionized labor, according to Netanyahu's plans, were to be cut down even more.

The plan included the reduction of the size of the public sector through downsizing and salary cuts as well as across-the-board budget cuts affecting all government ministries. Reforms in important economic sectors were announced, including the education system, pension funds, social security, energy, and telecommunications, as well as a tax reform program to stimulate domestic demand. Finally, the privatization of government-held companies was announced as a major goal. In practice, the government's main concern was unemployment and unemployment benefits. Accordingly, the plan sought, on the one hand, to toughen the criteria for unemployment benefits and reduce National Insurance benefits and, on the other hand, to improve the set of incentives in the labor market in order to raise the participation rate. The latter was to be achieved by the reduction of the number of foreign workers and the adoption of the "Wisconsin Plan" to encourage Israelis to move from welfare to work.

The attack on the welfare state and the public sector was matched by the announcement of a tax reform and the privatization of several large companies, such as the national airline and the refineries (companies with a stronger political clout, like the electrical company, were able to resist). Netanyahu's economic policies were highly praised by the business community in Israel and abroad. Coupled with the more relaxed security situation and the global recovery of the high-tech industry, the plan has led to economic growth (from −1.2 to 4.4 percent) and some reduction in unemployment, but has also increased the poverty rates and socioeconomic gaps. According to ADVA Annual Reports, in 2003 19.3 percent of households had a disposable income below poverty level, and their average income was 31 percent under the poverty line in 2003, on average, as opposed to 26 percent in 2001. In terms of inequality, the disposable income of the upper three deciles increased in real terms by 5–6 percent, while the disposable income of the first decile plunged by 9 percent. Real wages increased overall by 3.3 percent, but the minimum wage was not updated and decreased by about one percent of the average wage (from 48.8 percent of the average wage in 2003 to 47.2 percent in 2005).

The government's socioeconomic policy during the years 2002–3 contributed to a substantial increase in the extent of poverty and the deepening of the gaps in disposable income. The transfer of payments (as a percentage of the general income) decreased from 18.3 percent in 2002 to 17.5 percent in 2003 and to 16.2 percent in 2004. As a result, only 40 percent of poor families were extricated from poverty by the transfer payments, while the percentage of poor families in the population, based on their disposable income, reached 20.5 percent. This expansion in the extent of poverty occurred mainly as a result of acceleration in the depreciation of allowances and pensions, a development that hit families in the lower deciles more, whereas the income tax reform benefited the more affluent populations, who reaped the rewards of economic growth.

An inquiry committee appointed by the Knesset to study the increase of poverty reported,

> . . . an increase in the number of needy people applying to the services of charitable societies that provide food for the needy, soldiers who refrain from going home on leave on weekends, and students who are forced to miss classes on certain days, because they lack the bus fare or school books or need to help contribute to the family's income. All these factors create the feeling that the reality on the ground is deteriorating. Not only is there an increase in the incidence of poverty, but it appears that the poverty is deepening, and now we are talking about poverty that is not just proportionate, but there is real hunger, homelessness and a lack of basic learning equipment.[10]

[10] *Report and Survey of the Development of the Social Gaps in Israel in the Last Twenty Years.* Parliamentary Committee of Inquiry on the Issue of the Socio-economic Gaps in Israel, headed by M.K. Ran Cohen, Jerusalem, 2002, p. 22.

The elections in 2006 with the defeat of the Likud, including in its former strongholds in the periphery, have demonstrated the resentment neoliberalism evoked.

Conclusion

Israeli society has never lived up to its egalitarian image, as gaps between center and periphery and between ethnic groups have existed since its inception. Since 1980, however, the gaps have not only grown, but have been matched by a legitimating ideology of neoliberalism shared by the majority of the political parties. Israel's economic transformation since 1980 has turned it, on the one hand, into a Western-type globalized economy with a high-tech industry, a multinational labor force, and a thriving consumer culture. The same transformation, on the other hand, has turned Israel into a country with large gaps between rich and poor, with significant influence on the social cleavages described in chapter 1. Traditionally, economic preferences have had little influence on voting patterns in comparison to questions of peace in security. The 2006 elections, however, with the attempt of the Labor Party to adopt a social-democratic position and the neo-conservative agenda of the Likud might indicate that economic agendas will have greater influence in the future on Israeli politics and that the debate on economic policies has only just begun.

Acknowledgment

I would like to thank my research assistant, Omri Shamir, for his help.

Further Reading

ADVA Research Center www.adva.org.il

Aharoni, Y. 1998. "The changing political economy of Israel," *Annals of the American Political and Social Science* 555 (January), pp. 127–46

Bartram, D. V. 1998. "Foreign workers in Israel: history and theory," *International Migration Review* 32, 2, pp. 303–26

Ben-Porat, G. 2005. "Same old Middle East? The new Middle East and the *double* movement," *International Relations* 19, 1, pp. 39–62

Doron, A, and R. Kramer 1991. *The Welfare State in Israel – the Evolution of Social Security Policy and Practice*. Boulder: Westview Press

Doron, Gideon 1998. "The politics of mass communication in Israel," *Annals AAPSS* 555 (January), pp. 163–79

Peres, S. 1993. *The New Middle East*. New York: Holt

Ram, U. 2000. "The promised land of business opportunities: liberal post-Zionism in the Glocal age." In Shafir, G., and Y. Peled (eds.) 2000. *The New Israel: Peacemaking and Liberalization*. New York: Westview Press

Shalev M. 1992. *Labour and the Political Economy in Israel*, Oxford: Oxford University Press

Shalev, M. 1998. "Have globalization and liberalization 'normalized' Israel's political economy?" *Israel Affairs*, 5, 2–3, pp. 121–55

5

Military–Society Relations: the Demise of the "People's Army"

Yagil Levy

"The civilian is a soldier on eleven months' annual leave." That sentiment, expressed in the early 1950s by General Yigael Yadin, the second Chief of the General Staff of the Israel Defense Forces (IDF), has prevailed throughout Israel's history. Israelis have long viewed the IDF as more than simply the military; in popular mythology, the IDF is "the people's army," a crucial institution for both the defense of the state and the self-image of the nation. Nevertheless, the relationship between the Jewish-Israeli society and its army has been a tumultuous one. From its lofty status as a powerful "people's army" in the mid-1950s, the army has met with a succession of crises since the 1973 war, which intensified following its display of weakness in the First Lebanon War (1982–5) and the first Intifada (1987–93). These crises have led to a dilution of the army's resources, a reduction in its political support, a decline in its symbols, and even its gradual abandonment by social elites. The Al-Aqsa Intifada, the second major wave of violence between Israel and the Palestinians, which erupted in September 2000, filled the army's sails with fresh wind, though only temporarily. The Disengagement Plan (summer of 2005) placed the army once again in the midst of the political debate. Then the Second Lebanon War (summer of 2006) worsened the army's status. The prospect of replacing the drafted "people's army" with a voluntary-professional military, something not considered in the past, is now seriously discussed.

The People's Army

The French republican principle of the "citizen-soldier" was well assimilated in Israeli society. The IDF was founded along with the establishment of the state in 1948 and was organized on the basis of compulsory enlistment for every Jewish man and woman, the length of which settled in the 1970s at two years for women and three years for men. The army's core was a small regular army, consisting primarily of conscripts, with the officer corps and part of the professional echelon staffed by career personnel. A large reserve army was also established (inspired by the Swiss model), composed of conscripts obligated to do several weeks of reserve duty every year in order to maintain their fitness as soldiers in case of war. The standing army, according to this model, functions as the "manufactory" of the reserve army, as well as the initial forces assigned to curb an enemy's attack until mobilization of the reserves can be completed. This model facilitated a maximum extraction of manpower to reduce Israel's perceived inferiority to the Arab countries in both territorial and demographic terms, but without overburdening the civilian sectors, with the political costs that overburdening entails.

Political and military preparations for what was perceived as the inevitable "second round" of fighting became the cornerstone of politics, assuming that the military answer to that threat was the exclusive one. Israelis viewed the conflict with the Arab nations as a zero-sum game, in which Israel's defeat would deprive it of its survival as an independent entity. Hence, the "hard-line" school has always triumphed over the moderate ones, and diplomatic alternatives were ruled out. Against this background, Israel twice initiated pre-emptive strikes – the 1956 Suez War and the 1967 Six Day War – to eliminate what it had perceived as an existential threat posed by the neighboring Arabs. Of particular importance was the 1967 war, which ended with a massive Israeli victory, marked by the destruction of the fighting Arab armies and the conquest of large territories. After 1967 people felt more secure, and the idea that Israel was in danger of being wiped out was replaced by the motif of "security borders." This was a concept that eliminated existential danger and aggrandized Israel's military might, if only it would be allowed to preserve its new borders.

The centrality of war preparation and the glorious image of the IDF established its social centrality. This enabled the political leadership to use the IDF to establish internal control and authority beyond the army's instrumental missions. The model of a "nation in arms" was meshed with the model of state-building embraced by David Ben-Gurion, the state founder. It was a model characterized by a whole society ready for call-up, suspension of certain civil liberties, over-intrusiveness of state institutions, and a seemingly uniform Jewish-Western Israeli identity, devoid of ethnicity.

Under the wing of statism *(Mamlachtiyut)* – the state ideology that inculcated the idea that the state is a supreme entity, supplanting any particularist conception incompatible with state-directed goals – mass compulsory recruitment tied a Gordian knot between soldiering and citizenship in its most fundamental sense. Under the halo of the "people's army," this arrangement gave the army a favored symbolic status, and cultivated its image as a universal and depoliticized military that stands above society's sectarian divisions. Military service was not only a legal obligation imbued with symbolic meaning; it was also constructed in terms of social experience that determines the boundaries of society. So militarization ran its course: the perceived threat to Israel was discursively intensified and the army took on the roles of "nation builder" and "melting pot."

Ethnically, the IDF was consolidated and spearheaded by the dominant social group of middle-class, secular Ashkenazi men – the very group that had founded the army, populated its senior ranks, and that was identified with its achievements. The army was purportedly built on egalitarian foundations, although in fact, and as a by-product of its being shaped as a Western and modern army, the Ashkenazi secular group was designated to set the tone in terms of its quality. The Ashkenazi *warrior-Sabre* represented the dominant and proper (non-diasporic) masculinity of men who could pass the ultimate masculine test: combat.

Peripheral social groups, and in particular the Mizrachim, who had immigrated mainly from Arab countries in the state's early years, were portrayed as able to contribute to the army quantitatively, but not to shape its qualitative values. Women, who were deployed primarily in auxiliary roles, as well as standing as mothers at the forefront of the demographic (Jewish) struggle, were forced to the margins as well. Religious recruits were led by their fear of the secularizing influence of the army into auxiliary roles rather than a full military career. The exemption of other groups – Palestinian citizens and the young Ultra-Orthodox – from any kind of service distanced them from the construction site of the new Jewish Israeliness, and added to the value of those who did serve, especially Mizrachim.

Owing to the statism, military service became a decisive standard by which rights were awarded to individuals and collectives acting in the service of the state. Male Ashkenazi warriors, identified with the military's glorification, succeeded in translating their military dominance into legitimate social dominance. Military hierarchy definitively shaped the social hierarchy. At the same time, the IDF's very mass-based, universal conscription led to its perception as an interethnic "melting pot," as only in the military could all Israeli Jews meet on equal terms, without social barriers. Clearly, the ethos of the "melting pot" played a leading role in the state's absorption of the influx of Mizrachim and was instrumental in mitigating interethnic tensions.

The secular Ashkenazi group bore the burden of war for as long as it advanced its social status. Other groups – mainly Mizrachim, women, the national-religious, and, later on, immigrants from the former Soviet Union and Ethiopia – assimilated the principle of the citizen-soldier and its anticipated social rewards. This structure was, then, constituted on *materialist militarism*, that is military sacrifice for social rewards, at least by the 1980s.

The 1980s – After the Watershed

The Yom Kippur War of 1973 was the watershed after which the IDF's social status has seen a gradual decline. The war created a political opportunity, of which mass protest movements took advantage. The first wave of protest movements focused on supervising the military performance in the war in light of the "blunder." These activities were launched by protest groups of ex-reservists. Until then, the Israeli citizenry had not played an active role in monitoring military activities, but had passively tolerated military policies. After this protest the government established a judicial commission of inquiry (the Agranat Commission) to investigate the military's functioning in the war. The commission's findings led to the dismissal of several generals and ultimately to the resignation of Golda Meir's government. The protest helped, and was assisted by, the development of a press that became relatively independent from the political elites and gradually shifted its commitment from the ruling establishment to its reading/consuming public, to whom it felt primarily obliged. The first wave of protest followed the 1973 war and the second wave occurred at the end of the 1970s. Peace Now was the most notable organization involved. A mass movement of young, mainly Ashkenazi, ex-servicepersons led by officers in the reserves, it called on the government to exploit all political opportunities for peace.

But the most crucial turning point was the First Lebanon War. The Lebanon War was initiated by Israel in 1982 to eradicate the PLO-controlled quasi-state that had been formed in Southern Lebanon and that was perceived as a threat to the Israeli population living by the border (see chapter 1). The Begin government expanded the original goals, which had been partially agreed by the main political parties. In consequence, the IDF was forced to remain on south Lebanon's land for almost twenty more years, suffering heavy losses and withdrawing partially, in 1985, to a "security zone" established in Lebanon and then completely, in 2000, to the international border line. A similar scenario repeated itself during the Intifada that erupted in 1987 – the violent uprising by the Palestinians in the West Bank and the Gaza Strip against Israel's military rule. It became clear that the IDF had a limited capacity to contain the uprising, but not to annihilate it.

During the war in Lebanon, several new protest movements emerged and left their imprint on society–military relations. Yesh Gvul ("There is a limit/border"), organized reserve soldiers for the first time to selectively refuse to carry out military missions in Lebanon (and later in the occupied territories) because of the IDF's allegedly aggressive behavior. Other organizations, such as Soldiers Against Silence and Parents Against Silence, sprang up to protest against the extension of the war in Lebanon. By demanding an alternative to the accepted military way, these movements broadened their critical scope to include not only the army's modus operandum, but also its very purpose.

Central to this discourse was the unprecedented definition of the Lebanon War as a "war of choice" as distinct from the ostensible "wars of no choice" of the past, thus instilling the notion of an alternative to bellicosity. Largely as a result of these protests, the IDF partly and unilaterally withdrew from Lebanon in 1985. Additional protest groups followed, the most notable of which was Four Mothers, composed of parents of soldiers who had served in Lebanon, who demanded an immediate and complete withdrawal from this front in the middle of the 1990s. The effect of these movements' activity was to bring about restrictions, both direct and indirect, over the military's activity. Restrictions of this sort were increased after the outbreak of the first Intifada (1987), which brought the army into a political struggle for control over a population. This was a situation that threatened to fracture the ranks of the army, populated by soldiers from Israel's left and right wings. It also threatened to drive a wedge between military commanders and political forces, which were in conflict over the appropriate strategy for the army to adopt. Further cracks in the army's unity were caused by the nature of the soldiers' policing missions, which were seen increasingly as a failing struggle against a militarily inferior population. As a result, political protests were renewed with fresh energy, led by Peace Now and Yesh Gvul.

The Decline of State Militarism

The year 1973, and more notably the First Lebanon War, were the start of the decline of state militarism embodied in the Mamlachtiyut and the centrality of the "people's army." Four main processes were responsible for this shift, out of which the protest movements grew. The first was the significant increase in the use of social resources to maintain the Arab–Israeli conflict in the wake of the 1973 October war. This involved a considerable extension of military service: from 1970, compulsory service for males was extended from 30 to 36 months and the burden of reserve duty became 60 to 100 percent higher than the 1950–72 levels. In addition, there was a steep increase in defense spending, from about 10 percent of the GDP in the pre-1967 war period to about 23 percent in the years 1968–73, rising to about 28 percent from 1974 to 1980. Even though American aid alone covered about 40 percent of the defense budget, the rise in defense spending considerably exceeded GNP growth, in a way that increased the national debt. The state therefore failed to balance, as it had in previous wars, the security burden imposed on its citizens and the rewards they were provided with, especially as the 1973 war brought with it a financial crisis.

Second, the security burden became increasingly incongruent with the consumerist values growing in Israeli society from the late 1970s onward, generated by the rise in the standard of living produced by the 1967 Six Day War.

Third, the IDF's prestige declined as it demonstrated deficient prowess against Arab standing armies in the 1973 war and against Muslim militia in the Lebanon War, which eroded the prestige formerly conferred on military participants. In parallel, the diminishment of the external threat depleted the military sacrifice part of its value as a struggle over the very national existence. Concurrently, the army became a site for political clashes, especially when the dispute over the state's borders sharpened and disagreements over the army's conduct heightened.

Fourth, and crucial, were the cultural and economic globalization of Israeli society from the middle 1980s and the structural changes in the economy in the spirit of the neoliberal doctrines that were introduced (see chapter 4). Globalization strengthened the ethos of the market economy with its characteristic liberal discourse, which challenged the previous collectivist commitments and symbols. Prominent in the liberal agenda were new values such as individualism, privatization, competition, achievement, and efficiency. In this framework, violent conflict was portrayed as an obstacle in the way of Israel's participation in the global economy. Naturally, the market economy discourse also laid down the basis for an increasingly strident critique of the army's resources, as its budget was the largest single proportion of government spending. In practice, in the years 1980–2006, military spending as a proportion of GDP dropped by more than 50 percent, while GDP rose by about 200 percent, with most of the cutbacks directed at private consumption

The overall result of these four processes was the erosion of the army's role in defining the social hierarchy. The value of one's contribution to the state by means of military service was no longer necessarily the criterion that would determine the distribution of social goods and justify social domination, as individual achievement replaced the test of statism. Equally, groups that do not serve in the army, or who make a lesser contribution – such as the Ultra-Orthodox Jews, Palestinian citizens of Israel, and women – made certain achievements that were not dependent on the test of military service but rather were based on their own political power, wrapped in the liberal discourse of citizenship. Nothing was more symbolic of this than the decisions made by Yitzhak Rabin's government (in the early 1990s) to drop the requirement for military service as a basic condition for employment in the public sector, and to make the payment of child benefits no longer exclusive to ex-servicepersons.

Military service lost even more of its value as the vertical military hierarchy no longer provided the professional, value-based socialization required by an economy characterized by the emergence of flat-hierarchy high-tech organizations. Reserve duty also became a heavier burden in both absolute and relative terms, and it began to hamper reserve soldiers both from effectively contending in an increasingly competitive labor market, and from fulfilling their roles as fathers within a more equal division of labor in the family. In short, competition was arising between the "military time" and the "civilian time."

The "Motivation Crisis"

Alongside protest activities, the change in orientation among the secular Ashkenazi middle class could be seen in the form of pressure to lessen military sacrifice or to increase the rewards for it. One mode of action was reflected in the cultivation of internal pressures of various kinds to divert resources from military reinforcement to private consumption (including reducing tax burdens). This reduced investment in security (as a proportion of GDP) from a peak of 31 percent in 1974–6 to around 17 percent in 1986–90 and around 10 percent during the 1990s.

A second mode of action could be seen in the gradual forsaking of the army, and especially a reduction in motivation for combat duty – the "motivation crisis" syndrome, as some aspects of this were termed in public discourse during the middle of the 1990s. This trend had a number of aspects: a slow and continual decline in general willingness to enlist, and particularly to enlist in combat units; fewer volunteers for officer training; a rise in the number of potential recruits purposely trying to alter their medical profile – which determines the soldier's qualification to perform his/her duties – as a means to avoid combat duty (see also chapter 6); a rise in the number of enlistees requesting to serve at a base close to their home; and a significant increase in the number of young people dropping out before and during their service, ostensibly on mental health grounds. Secular Ashkenazim were at the forefront of this crisis, joined by the upwardly mobile Mizrachim, who adopted a pattern of motivation similar to that of the secular Ashkenazim. Among the latter, the collective agricultural sector – the kibbutzim and moshavim, who were symbolically identified with having made a vital contribution to the IDF was especially affected by the erosion of the IDF's status following Lebanon, and displayed attenuated motivation.

The state exacerbated the motivation crisis by its own actions. Not only did it contribute to the erosion of symbolic rewards by directing the IDF to politically disputed missions in Lebanon and the territories, it also began to reform the conscription system from being inclusionist to selective. Two processes are particularly worth mentioning. First, in 1985 the reserve army was reformed and the burden of reserve duty was reduced. The main thrust of the reform was gradually to transfer the cost of reserve duty from the National Insurance Institute to the army. Previously, the daily cost of a reserve soldier (primarily compensating him/her for loss of earnings) was not borne by the security budget, and so the reserve army was managed largely in isolation from economic considerations. The reform provided an incentive for the army to rein in its usage of reservists and to divert resources to other purposes. This process was part of a broad cutback in the security budget in the framework of the "Economic Stability Plan," which, in 1985, eliminated the hyper-inflation, and heralded the gradual shift to a "market society" (see chapter 4). Indeed, beyond its budgetary implications, the reform meant that the reserves began to be managed according to the perquisites of the market economy, and a price tag was attached to the service of reserve soldiers. This resulted in a dramatic reduction in the number of overall reserve duty days, and an easing of the burden of reserve duties. To illustrate: in 2001, reserve duty was funded on the basis of 3.8 million days per year instead of 10 million in 1985, before the reform. At the same time, the number of days served by reservists dropped from an average of 26 days per year in 1990, to 16 in 2000. On top of that, only a small percentage of the population participates in a significant reserve service. In short, the reform of the reserves brought about for the first time a semi-selective recruitment model, which deviated from the universalist principles of an inclusive "people's army."

However, this is a case of trying to right one wrong with another: the army's inefficiency, characterized by the wasteful recruitment of reservists, was resolved by increasing inequality in the reserves. The cutback in reserve duty days weighed most heavily on combat units, where the middle class was bearing most of the burden, in terms of both the reservists and their employers. The burden placed on non-combat forces, with their larger representation of other social strata, was lightened as reserve duty days were reduced and cheaper, civilian alternatives to reservists were found. A new contradiction thus emerged from the directives of the market economy: economic savings for the army at the cost of an increased financial burden on the middle class, itself already faced with a high tax burden and the contradictory pressures of the market economy. Consequently, from the middle of the 1990s, reservists were organized to claim their rights, as detailed below.

Second, selectivity encompassed the compulsory army as well. Numerically speaking, the defection of secular Ashkenazim, together with the expansion of the non-military Torah-study route (see more below), and the disqualification of poorly educated draftees, largely owing to the growing human reservoir following the mass immigration in the 1990s from the former Soviet Union, led to a reduction in recruitment rates: since the year 2000 less than 60 percent of Jewish men have been serving full military service, and this number continues to drop.

Naturally, growing selectivity amplified the enlisted persons' bargaining power with the IDF, especially as selectivity also cracked the military's image as an inclusionist "people's army," the boundaries of which overlaid those of the Israeli-Jewish community, and thus further devalued its status. Several patterns of bargaining can thus be observed.

Personal bargaining: Since the 1990s, soldiers have begun to negotiate with the army in person or via their families or other networks. These negotiations can determine the individual's role in the army, the conditions under which he/she serves, restrictions on his/her service and military function, and even the very fact of his/her serving at all. The strengthening of liberal values and their partial infiltration into modes of action among governmental institutions, have empowered the individual's standpoint and put him/her in a stronger negotiating position, sometimes with the assistance of the legal system. The media has featured many stories of artists, athletes, and models who chose not serve in the military, as it would interfere with their careers.

Military parenting: This can be seen in the increasing and quite open involvement of parents in affairs of the army. Parents, among them bereaved parents, even get involved in matters such as training accidents, operational accidents, the political justification of missions, and military service conditions. This involvement is effective because many of the parents are themselves army veterans or reservists who "know the system."

The political selection of missions: This can be seen in the strengthening of the phenomena of both explicit and selective, and "gray" conscientious objection, and the appearance of political movements that ideologically endorse it.

Economic bargaining: Military duties became conditional on economic remuneration. The most striking illustration is the "revolts" in the late 1990s among reservists (such as pilots) arising from a lack of insurance cover, and consumerist-style associations of reserve soldiers demanding easier conditions, as well as appropriate financial compensation for their service. Pressure to increase the monetary rewards for reservists and their employers were partially answered by improved compensation for reservists (especially those serving for longer periods of time).

Redistributional bargaining: This involved pressure to redistribute the burden, especially the demand in the 1990s to recruit yeshiva students. It was a rearguard action to piece together the remnants of the republican principle of civic duty, if not by increasing the rights of those who bore the burden or negating the rights of those who did not, then by making greater demands on the latter. Amendments to legislation only partially met this demand, however.

To a large extent, these patterns of bargaining embodied a retreat from "obligatory militarism," which sees compulsory military service as an unconditional contribution to the state, and the adoption of "contractual militarism," that is, making service conditional on its meeting the individual's ambitions and interests. The very activity of protest groups and the "motivation crisis" undermined the status of militarism in Israel. At the same time, demilitarization found its expression in the opening of a new cultural space for voices challenging the centrality of the military and the state of war in Israeli's experience.

The State's Response

This interlocked process – protest, de-militarization, and the motivation crisis – produced two contradictory effects along two different life cycles. While the long-term effect was a realignment of the social composition of the IDF, the short-term effect was to reduce military control over human and material resources, thus limiting the military's freedom of action in the realm of statecraft. The more the political disputes over the use of military force intensified, the more Israel's capacity to use force declined because the state bureaucracy and the military establishment had to calculate carefully the expected political outcomes. Accordingly, Israeli statecraft, in which the military had long played a central role, was channeled into non-military pursuits.

The visible result was the de-escalation of the Israeli–Arab conflict – that is the level of friction between Israel and its Arab neighbors was reduced so that the level of social investment in security, in both material and human terms, reflected the fact that military sacrifice was perceived as less legitimate than it had been before. The IDF, protective of its internal integration, social status, and its decreasing human and material resources, found itself being driven increasingly to adjust to a civilian set of considerations, under pressure from civilian groups. It was precisely because it was a "people's army," with the resources, prestige, and the professional mobility of the officer corps in the civilian labor market that this status entails, that the IDF was sensitive to shifts in the profile of the social legitimacy it enjoyed. The IDF therefore cooperated with the political powers in managing de-escalation. In addition to attempting to cool down the conflict, the government and the army were geared to divert resources (including legitimation) from the Egyptian conflict to the Palestinian one, through which the main battle over the "Land of Israel" would be determined.

The first move was the peace treaty signed with Egypt in 1979 at the price of Israel's full withdrawal from the Sinai Peninsula. Central to this move was the IDF's interest in decreasing its human and material costs by eliminating the Egyptian threat and gaining American aid to help rebuild the army. Nonetheless, the government reversed the de-escalation process by launching the First Lebanon War. A battle against a demonic (PLO), yet inferior enemy, could have annulled the effects of the 1973 war on the IDF's position as much as it could have defeated the Palestinian national spirit, had it ended with a glorious and swift victory. But the war concluded with the withdrawal of most of the exhausted Israeli forces from Lebanon in 1985, under political pressure by protest groups but in return for generous American aid, and was accompanied by a cut in the defense budget and the downsizing of the military industries. Later, the Labor Party under Yitzhak Rabin displayed greater flexibility than the previous Likud-dominated government in taking advantage of international and regional developments (the fall of the Soviet Union and Iraq's defeat in the Gulf War), which weakened the PLO's power alongside the IDF's inability to rule the Palestinians militarily. The result was an acceleration of the diplomatic processes, with the Oslo Agreement (1993) at the center. Resentment of the human and material costs of war also played a role in Israel's unilateral and complete withdrawal from Lebanon in 2000 and in the military's support for diplomatic overtures with Syria in 1992–2000.

However, the demilitarization and the peace process, which involved territorial concessions, gave rise to a counter-reaction amongst peripheral and religious groups, just as they eroded the IDF's social and autonomous status and motivated it to rehabilitate its position. So, the strategy of demilitarization could only be an interim rather than a long-term measure, which helped to reduce pressures from the political leadership and the IDF. Thus, the second contradictory effect, a long-term one, was a change in the military's social composition, which also empowered the army to resume belligerency.

The Ethno-National Challenge

With, on the one hand, the declining interest of the elites in military service and, on the other hand, the downturn in the image of the omnipotent Ashkenazi *warrior-Sabre* in wars, other groups were able to enter the political scene and challenge, directly and indirectly, the hegemonic military symbols. The *ethno-national ethos* was at the center of the challenges issued by the more peripheral groups. Ethnonationalism strengthened in response to the aftermath of the Six Day War, in which the Israeli-Jewish community renewed its encounter with historically venerated sites such as the Old City of Jerusalem and Hebron. For religious and rightist cycles, the occupation was a stimulus to reassert their identification with Jewish tradition (see chapters 1 and 2). Traditional Judaism, which invoked the primordial in the building of the Israeli-Jewish community, became for many a crucial factor in re-demarcating the boundaries of Israeli society.

In this way, citizenship came to be based not on individual rights deriving from the individual's belonging formally to the state, but on rights rooted in the membership of a collective community, whose primordial identity was Jewish. Groups expected to achieve status by merely belonging to the Jewish collective – status was no longer seen as dependent on historical or contemporary contributions, military or otherwise, as had been associated with Ashkenazi dominance and legitimized by the statist, republican discourse. This led to the

Mamlachtiyut-informed republican ethos being challenged not only by the liberal, market-oriented discourse, described in chapter 4, but also by an ethno-national discourse. Introduced originally by the Likud and Gush Emunim, the ethno-national discourse became a magnet for less mobile Mizrachi and religious groups – who had been marginalized and thereby alienated by statism – and offered them unconditional, meaningful partnership in shaping the "common good" of the Jewish-Israeli community.

In the spirit of this change, the main type of challenge to the Ashkenazi hegemony in the army was posited by groups who had been disappointed by their inability to gain the recognition or attain a worthy status in the army, namely Shas, a Mizrachi Ultra-Orthodox movement. Set up in the 1980s, Shas successfully demanded that yeshiva students' exemption from military service would increase but at the same time would not be at the cost of the privileges awarded to ex-servicepersons. This presented an alternative to the centrality of the army and the Gordian knot that had been tied between soldiering and citizenship. Shas contributed to the institutionalization of the military exemption given to yeshiva students under the heading of *Torato Omanuto* ("the study of Torah is his livelihood"). It made a political commitment to uphold the exemption and even to expand it.

The exemption of Orthodox men from the army was a part of the religious–secular status quo established in pre- and early statehood (see chapter 1). A few hundred young people were exempted in the early years of the state, as Ben-Gurion's gesture to the Ultra-Orthodox rabbinate during the early 1950s towards rebuilding the Orthodox yeshivas after the devastation of the Holocaust. In the 1990s this number climbed to around 10 percent of potential recruits. Furthermore, Shas refused to bow down to hegemonic secular militarism as the Ashkenazi Ultra-Orthodox parties did, instead unhesitatingly presenting the route of studying Torah as no less worthy, if not more so, than the military one. Shas thus constructed an alternative pattern of rewards for an increasingly Ultra-Orthodox population in the form of a huge project of Mizrachi yeshivas. This route offered greater material and symbolic rewards than military participation, which, for such young people, had meant either "dropping out" or taking a marginal position in the blue-collar segments of the military. However, the ethno-national groups not only challenged the Ashkenazi hegemony in discourse and politically; they also increased their practical hold on the IDF.

The "Army of the Peripheries"

Five groups (hereafter referred to as the "new groups"), which had previously been relegated to a peripheral status in the army's ranks, came to fill the vacuum created by the secular Ashkenazi middle class's partial abandonment of combat units: Mizrachim – at first the relatively socially mobile Mizrachim, and later the less mobile ones; the national religious youth; new immigrants, mainly those from the former Soviet Union and Ethiopia; Druze and Bedouin citizens of Israel; and, more slowly, women. This change in the army's composition began in the 1980s, although it sped up during the 1990s alongside the Oslo Process and the withdrawal from Lebanon.

These new groups perceived the army as a sphere in which they could construct new routes of mobility and legitimately attain various civil rights, whilst proving that they too were capable of the elite groups' achievements in combat. This was quite often a direct challenge to Ashkenazi secular dominance. As many of their members held ethno-national values, these groups viewed military duties as a means to fulfill their ideological values by protecting the borders of the "Greater Land of Israel" against the perceived hostility of the Arab world.

While the Ashkenazi and Mizrachi middle class reformulated their military contribution and gradually staffed positions in the elite and the sophisticated technological units, the new groups increasingly staffed "blue-collar" combat positions in greater numbers, in the following ways.

Women: The lack of high-quality manpower, as defined by IDF officers, was instrumental in the advancement of women in the army. Demands from women's organizations, and the "motivation crisis," spurred on the army to expand the recruitment of women, who, until the 1980s, had been restricted to auxiliary roles. Field positions had been slowly opened up to women since the First Lebanon War, and women were gradually being given greater access to combat roles. The watershed was Alice Miller's petition to the High Court of Justice in 1995. The court accepted her complaint regarding the rejection of her application to the pilot training course, and these courses were consequently opened up to women. In 2003 it was decided that women serving in combat positions would have to serve for 36 months, like their male counterparts, instead of 24 months.

The Mizrachim: The army was relatively open to Mizrachim from the 1980s onwards, though their mode of integration reflected changes in their internal stratification. The most mobile Mizrachi groups, who entered the upper ladders of the middle class, had internalized the republican principle from the outset, understanding that military service was a tool for social mobility, and accordingly deepened their hold on the army. However, during the 1990s, many Mizrachim began to attain mobility in the middle class without regard to their military achievements, thus devaluing the significance of military service. Mizrachi youth from the upper echelons of the middle class began to adopt similar attitudes to their Ashkenazi friends: in other words, their motivation towards the army declined. On the other hand, for Mizrachi youth from the lower strata of the middle class, military service remained an important test of citizenship. In fact, these Mizrachi renewed the traditional military ethos of the sacrificial service elite. This could be seen as an act of defiance in the face of the secular Ashkenazi service elite, and – in operational terms – led to this group's increased presence in combat units and among officers. Mizrachim, then, were "climbing down the escalator" – increasing their grasp on senior positions while these steps forward were paralleled by a devaluation of the military status.

Immigrants from the former Soviet Union: In a similar way to the Mizrachim, immigrants from the former Soviet Union saw military service as a symbolic "entrance pass" into Israeli society, and even as a test for gaining formal citizenship. This also applied to Christian immigrants (who came to Israel as part of mixed-religion families), who found the army to be a fast and convenient route for converting to Judaism, or at least an entry point to Israeli society based on their military contribution. Immigrants from the 1990s exploited the "motivation crisis" to gain promotion through the ranks. By the early years of the twenty-first century this group comprised about 20 percent of the ground forces.

Immigrants from Ethiopia: For young immigrants from Ethiopia, military service not only provided access to an Israeli identity, but was also a way of improving their self-confidence and even finding a certain feeling of superiority over their counterparts. This was based on their self-image as more self-disciplined soldiers, who were prepared to serve far from their family homes, and to accept the military hierarchy.

The Druze and Palestinian citizens: From the 1980s the IDF began to make a greater effort to persuade Bedouins – who were separated from the Palestinian minority and not subject to the draft – to volunteer for combat duty – and not only to serve as trackers, which had been their traditional role in the military. These efforts resulted in the establishment (in the early 1990s) of a patrol battalion that served during the Intifada on Israel's border with the Palestinian Authority in the area of Rafah in the Gaza Strip. The Bedouins' motivation was manifold: an ambition to attain equal rights through signing up to the army; an attraction to military activities, channeled into serving in the IDF; and seeing service in the army as a profession at a time of unemployment and economic instability. For the state and the army, recruiting the Bedouins was not only a way of dealing with a lack of manpower but also an attempt at holding back increased Islamization among that group.

Men from the Druze community are subject to compulsory recruitment, and from the 1990s some of the restrictions regarding their service were lifted, and they began to be integrated into combat units alongside Jewish soldiers. For the Druze, unlike the Bedouins, fighting the Palestinians is a tool in shaping an Israeli, and not an Arab, identity. In return, the state provides preferential rewards in comparison to those offered to Palestinian citizens of Israel.

The religious: A major part of the army's changing social architecture could be seen in the increasing number of "knitted skullcaps" in the army from the 1980s onwards, central to which was the gradual cognizance among religious Zionist youth that the time had come to lay down a challenge to the secular Ashkenazi nation-founding stratum. The foundation of the *yeshivot hesder* ("arrangement academies") – a special program, begun in 1965, that enabled Torah study in a yeshiva alongside combat service in homogeneously religious companies – helped to overcome the rabbis' earlier reticence, which centered on an anxiety that religious youth would be exposed to the secularizing influence of the army. For this group, the main symbolic return for military participation was carrying out the mission of the renewal of the Jewish hold in the perceived holy lands. To a large extent, the settlement project in the West Bank by Gush Emunim, which was imbued with religious meaning, turned Ashkenazi religious Zionism from a marginal sector, before the 1970s, into a central political and cultural stream. The increased recruitment to the army formed a complementary layer to the activity of Gush Emunim, which after the 1973 war had ideologically led the Jewish settlement project in the West Bank (see also chapters 1–3).

This process expanded after the First Lebanon War and coincided with the "motivation crisis" discussed on pp. 124–7. Gradually, more and more settlers of the West Bank and Gaza Strip joined the ranks. As the numbers of religious combat soldiers grew, their rabbis had a stronger position of power from which to negotiate with the army to gain influence on the army's values and leverage to enable their military service to fulfill their ideological mission.

The Political Impact of a Multicultural Army

With the change in the army's social composition, military service gradually came to be based on social groups who had internalized the fundamentals of military culture and were supportive of the army's role in the territories and elsewhere. In contrast, the criticism of the IDF and the restrictions placed on its functioning after 1980 were largely the result of secular Ashkenazi organizational activities. These organizations strove to subject the army's behavior to a logic that was at least partially non-military, and even when it was military, it contradicted the army's organizational rationale. This formed the common ground of movements such as Peace Now, Yesh Gvul, Soldiers Against Silence, and Four Mothers. The IDF therefore played an active role in creating arrangements that would actually make the army a multicultural site and thus encourage members of the new groups to join the forces.

In order to minimize politicization of the ranks, and in attempt to remain in consensus, the army began to remove reservists from friction zones. The First Lebanon War laid bare the political collapse of the model of a middle-class-based reserve army. The middle class levered its military participation into political involvement – mainly in the shape of protest organizations – which contributed to the fracturing of the army's professional autonomy. The lesson that had been learnt was implemented in Lebanon from 1985 to 2000, as the fighting was increasingly carried out by the conscript army, which was easier to control. A similar pattern was repeated successfully during the Al-Aqsa Intifada.

The ethno-class stratification of the IDF, unlike in other armies, is considered a taboo subject. Indeed, in keeping with the discourse that portrays the "people's army" as being above ethno-class divisions in Israeli society, no official statistics are available regarding the representation of different groups. Although the IDF's claim to a "people's army" is no longer tenable, as less than 60 percent of the Jewish population completes military service, the army clings to the rhetoric and doctrine of the "people's army," the source of its preferential status in Israeli society. Mapping the casualties in the Al-Aqsa Intifada provided an indication of the change in the social composition of the army since the first week of the First Lebanon War (June 1982), in which most of the military forces, both regular soldiers and reservists, were active.

In the first week of the Lebanon War, about 48 percent of those killed were secular Ashkenazim, who had previously manned core positions in the military. In contrast, in the Al-Aqsa Intifada, only about 28 percent of the fatalities came from these groups, with soldiers from the more peripheral and religious groups taking their place. If we calculate the fatality rates of the core of the secular middle class – the Ashkenazi groups together with the Mizrachi middle class – the drop is from about 68 percent to around 46 percent, while the demographic weight of these groups remained almost stable, so demography alone may not account for this change. This picture was repeated in the Second Lebanon War, with the exception that the kibbutz youth increased their share. Part of this trend resulted from the efforts by the kibbutz movement's leaders to counter the decline of this group in the IDF and the kibbutz youth's over-presence in the still attractive elite units, which were overburdened in the war.

The change in the casualties map gave the army more room for maneuver in the direction of autonomous action. By the time the Al-Aqsa Intifada erupted in September 2000 at the Palestinian initiative – following the failure to arrive at a final agreement during the Camp David talks in the summer of 2000 – the army's composition was based mainly on the new groups. As a result, the IDF could deploy force with renewed legitimacy. Indeed, the army systematically acted to escalate its response to the uprising by excessive response to the Palestinian hostilities, thus leading to many Palestinian casualties and to the collapse of the Palestinian Authority. A peace coalition, which might have attempted to curb the IDF politically, energized by protests flourishing from within the military ranks, as in previous wars, did not emerge. Given that the instigators of political protest were mainly ex-soldiers, especially reservists, and their families, the social realignment had a crucial effect on the reshaping of the bereavement ethos, from protest, which typified the First Lebanon War, to the acceptance of the sacrifice submissively, with conciliation, forgiveness, and even pride.

Even if this was not its intention at the outset, the army saw in the conflict with the Palestinians a good opportunity to halt the decline of its lofty social status. Just before the Intifada the IDF had hurriedly and unilaterally retreated from Lebanon on the government's orders, with the Hezbollah's militias snapping at its heels. Moreover, since the middle of the 1990s the army had been dealing with the "motivation crisis." And as if this were not enough, not only did the army's primary mission – fighting in Lebanon – come to an end, but this itself intensified the "threat" that the market economy would eat away at the army's resources; and indeed, the budget proposal of the year 2001 included a relatively deep cutback in the army's spending. The first years of the Al-Aqsa Intifada tempered this decline and put it on hold. Nonetheless, even the Intifada was not effective in entirely deflecting this process, which led to the Disengagement Plan.

The Disengagement Plan

In 2003 the army could point to real achievements in reducing the number of terrorist attacks carried out by Palestinian organizations. Paradoxically, this was also the year that saw a rise in public criticism over the IDF's performance in the occupied territories. Two years later, the result was the unilateral withdrawal from the Gaza Strip and the north of the West Bank in what was termed the "Disengagement Plan."

A combination of several challenges was at the center of the decline in the army's legitimacy. Critical was the erosion of the legitimacy of the army's financial and human resources indicated by the upper-middle class's (direct and indirect) pressure to cut the defense budget and to reform the conscription model in a way that would reduce the burden. Consequently, in 2004, while the IDF was fighting, the government ratified cuts in the budget, while simultaneously providing tax relief to the benefit of the middle class and above. Later, in 2005, the government adopted a reform plan that would reduce the load on army reserve soldiers by reducing the exemption age to forty, deploying reserves in emergencies only, shortening the period of service, and releasing thousands of soldiers from the service. A similar reform was adopted with regard to compulsory service in an attempt to gradually shorten it from three to two years.

The legitimacy of fighting was eroded at the same time. Israel's increasing globalization brought with it openness to the normative judgments passed by global institutions. Limits in the use of force were more deeply recognized with growing criticism of the IDF's conduct in the occupied territories. Normative restrictions were then increasingly placed on the use of firearms, such as house destruction, conduct at roadblocks, air bombing in civilian concentrations, several practices of policing and more. In addition, the years 2003–4 saw the strengthening of the refusal movement, not necessarily in terms of numbers, but qualitatively, first, in the shape of the higher-ranking officers and members of elite units who joined the movement and, second, in high-profile media coverage of the movement.

These trends gradually narrowed the army's freedom of action once more, and, in particular, reduced its resources, thereby increasing the need to find alternative modes of fighting/policing. Against this background the IDF cooperated with the political leadership in carrying out the withdrawal from the Gaza Strip, with the evacuation of the Jewish settlements serving as a model that would decrease the IDF's friction with the Palestinian population and the costs involved in protecting the settlements. Politically, the army joined the "no partner" thesis of mainstream Israeli politics that underscored the unilateral initiatives.

Over the course of one week in the summer of 2005, the IDF unprecedentedly evacuated thousands of Jewish settlers from the Gaza Strip and the northern West Bank. The army's evacuation tactics relied on the concentration of large forces of soldiers in the settlements being evacuated, creating a significant relative quantitative advantage for the army over the settlers, who were expected to oppose their evacuation aggressively. Furthermore, not only was the evacuation swift, but the army maintained the unity of its ranks, even in executing a politically controversial mission. Early predictions that the evacuation of settlements would result in massive refusals within the army's ranks, mainly among the national religious conscripts who identified with the settlement project, proved completely false.

It could be argued that the effective functioning of the army rested largely on the religious networks' interests in preserving their mobility within the IDF's ranks. Mass refusal accompanied by violent clashes between the army and the uprooted settlers (whose youth gradually seized positions within the ground forces) would have endangered the achievements the "knitted skullcaps" had accomplished since the 1980s and would raise questions about the ability of the group to continue to deepen its hold on the army and rise to the very top, in the spirit of the group's leadership.

Despite, or maybe owing to, the IDF's effective performance, the Disengagement distanced from the army a section of the religious recruits, for whom the destruction of the settlement enterprise threatened to return religious Zionism to the status of a sector and thus also threatened the identity of considerable numbers of the conscripts. A new form of "motivation crisis," this time among the religious, was monitored at several levels.

The Civil Agenda and the Second Lebanon War

The Disengagement coincided with the trend towards de-escalation to generate a renewal of the "civil agenda." More than ever, this agenda threatened to cut back the IDF's resources and divert part of the defense budget to welfare or tax cuts. Significantly, following the elections of 2006, the most civilian leadership in Israel's history took the reins, with Ehud Olmert as prime minister and Amir Peretz, the former leader of the Hisatdrut and a dovish politician, as a defense minister. The term "civilian," related not only to the background of the leaders but to their political agenda as well – i.e., the "convergence plan" of withdrawal from most of the West Bank and the cutback in the defense budget. However, it was the "civilian" leadership that retaliated to the abduction of two reserve soldiers by the Hezbollah in July 2006 with a large-scale operation that escalated into the Second Lebanon War.

This month-long war, in which Israel launched massive airstrikes on the Lebanese civilian infrastructure while Hezbollah launched Katyusha rockets into northern Israel, gradually escalated to include the city of Haifa. As Israel's much-hyped high-tech army failed to stop Katyusha rockets from landing in its cities, a ground invasion of southern Lebanon took place. After a month, the UN brokered a ceasefire resolution and the war ended with the deployment of the Lebanese army and a multinational force along the border.

This war ended, more than any past war, with a strong public sense that the IDF had failed in its mission. The civilian population had suffered heavier casualties and damage (which, of course, were dramatically lower than that of the Lebanese population) than at any time since the 1948 war, and the IDF had seemed ineffective at preventing it. Ground clashes between the IDF and the Hezbollah forces further exposed the IDF's weakness, inflicting heavy losses, and revealing the low level of the forces' preparedness and the command's performance. The embroilment of the IDF in a long "policing war" in the occupied territories, which distanced it from the real battlefield, the regular cutback in its resources, the gap between the legitimacy of using force and the legitimacy of investing resources in the use of force, which resulted in hesitancy in calling up the reserves and launching the ground operation, and finally the failure to acknowledge the limitations in using force, were among the factors contributing to the IDF's malfunction.

In sharp contradiction to the Al-Aqsa Intifada, organizations of reservists and bereaved families engineered the protests that brought about the appointment of a government committee to investigate the war. For multiple reasons, the army in effect gave up on the reserve system in its traditional form and granted low priority to training and equipping reservists. When the war erupted and the reserve divisions were mobilized and hesitantly sent to fight for ambiguous goals, it became apparent that the IDF simply violated the "psychological contract" established with the reservist. Within the terms of this contract, the reservist is always ready to be called up, while the IDF's part is to ensure that the reservist will be trained, equipped, and utilized effectively. The IDF and its political supervisors thereby lost part of the autonomy they had regained during the Al-Aqsa Intifada.

The Political Supervision of the IDF

Complaints regarding the weakness of civilian control of the army are often heard in the public and academic discourse in Israel. Nevertheless, a study of the political–military relations in Israel reveals an apparent paradox: within a period of about seventy years, the more the militarization of Israeli society and politics increased, the more successful politicians were in institutionalizing effective control over the IDF. Militarization passed through three main stages: (1) accepting the use of force as a legitimate political instrument during the pre-state period (1920–48); (2) giving this instrument priority over political-diplomatic means in the state's first years up to the point in which (3) military discourse gradually predominated over political discourse after the 1967 war. Each stage was accompanied by a gradual increase in resources devoted to war preparation and an amplification of force-oriented preferences reflected in foreign policies. Even ostensibly diplomatic arrangements, the most important of which were the Oslo Accords, were formulated in military terms.

At the same time, political control over the IDF was tightened. Inculcation of the principle of subordination of the armed forces to the political leadership during the pre-state period gave way to the construction of formal and informal restraints on autonomous military action. During the 1980s the principle of political control over the army was further institutionalized when a state commission of inquiry held the political powers liable for the massacre perpetrated by the Christian phalange in the Palestinian refugee camps of Sabra and Shatila in Beirut, and forced Defense Minister Ariel Sharon to resign. Other areas (such as the defense budget) were later monitored, with greater involvement of the Knesset and civilian agencies.

The militarization of politics has contributed greatly to this monitoring of the army. It has made the army interested in being portrayed as a universal, apolitical organization that does the government's bidding, and has created a dependence on the political leadership as the army's supplier of resources. And, paradoxically, the very increase of military figures taking up eminent positions in politics, has contributed to the tightening of operative control over the IDF. Fewer and fewer spheres of military action have remained autonomous or hidden from the public eye. Institutional monitoring by civilian agencies has become much more powerful since the First Lebanon War, and has been backed up by public monitoring, as social movements have stepped into the arena. Assisted by the press, groups such as soldiers' parents and reservists have amplified their scrutiny of traditionally professional issues, thus undermining the IDF's autonomy at several levels. This has included journalists' and parents' investigations of accidents in military operations and training; reservists' critique of the distribution of the military burden, generating legislative attempts at limiting the IDF's powers to call up reservists; homosexuals' and women's successful struggle to lift limitations on their military promotion; press scrutiny of budgets, nominations, and military performance; and more. While previous political supervision of the army had been mainly concerned with formal, institutional aspects, from this point on it also took the form of wider public supervision carried out by social groups.

Nevertheless, militarization means the supremacy of military thinking over political-civilian thinking. In other words, the military view of political reality has become the main anchor of Israeli statesmanship. Consequently, though the army became subjected to "over-surveillance" by civilian institutions, these institutions were not provided with more capacity to prevent military escalation that does not serve political goals. As Israel's political-military history since the 1980s indicates, the army did not rebel in a determined fashion against the authority of the political echelon, but rather took advantage of its weakness (as during the Al-Aqsa Intifada when the political leadership explicitly refrained from enforcing restraint over the IDF), or exploited the freedom of action afforded it by politicians on the grounds of the primacy of political military thinking.

Forecasting Premises

It is safe to predict that in the near future the military will continue to maintain, at least in part, its centrality in the Jewish-Israeli society, whether because of the collective memory of its central position in the past or the visibility of the friction between Israel and the Arab world. To a large extent, the IDF will face the typical difficulties of functioning in a "twilight zone" of neither full-scale war nor full peace. Similarly, it seems safe to envisage a consistent decline in the scope of military participation and of defense expenditure despite the trend of temporary resource increases after wars. The gradual shift to a selective draft and the possibility that conscription will be abolished altogether in the fairly near future are the main options that are predicted. As discussed, since the late 1990s the IDF has shifted to a semi-selective model of conscription, although the mandatory service has not been formally ended. With the reforms in the conscription model and the aftermath of the Disengagement and the Second Lebanon War, this trend will intensify. Simply put, the IDF has gradually and systematically lost the confidence of various groups since the turning point of the 1980s: the Ashkenazi upper-middle class in the politically disputed First Lebanon War and the first Intifada, the national religious groups in the Disengagement, and the middle-class reservists in the Second Lebanon War. It is reasonable to assume that in the wake of these wars, the erosion of confidence will increase the difficulty of drafting and activating the reserves.

With the drying up of the valuable symbolic rewards that the IDF can offer to its recruits, the professionalization of the IDF seems the most likely avenue. Professionalization would provide the army with several advantages: (1) a trade-off between increased monetary rewards, claimed by both reservists and conscripts, and decreased personnel; (2) professionalization of ranks by basing the model on service by relatively few, for relatively long periods, to ensure that they maintain fitness, in return for monetary compensation; (3) de-politicization of the ranks by "purchasing" services rather than recruiting soldiers, thus mitigating previous ethical orientations. Soldiers of this "professional army" would not suffer from pangs of conscience when carrying out their assignments.

In common with the experience of other Western armies, the realignment of the social composition of the IDF toward further reliance on religious and peripheral may aggravate the militarization of the ranks. A volunteer army would draw the bulk of its personnel from Israel's lower middle class and religious sectors. Material rewards, the potential for professional and social mobility, and militaristic values already attract more recruits from these groups to the military than from other parts of the population. Ending conscription would sharpen that bias. The result could be an army filled primarily by politically conservative groups, providing the familiar linkage between lower-class position, religious, and rightist orientations. The predominance of these groups in the army would inevitably heighten militarism and aggravate tension between the IDF high command and civilian elites, who would distance themselves from the army and the implications of its aggressive actions.

This implies a contradiction between the military as a magnet for the peripheral groups and its gradual decline as a central institution in the perception of the dominant social class. While the middle-class groups are likely to distance themselves from the IDF and to seek to decrease its resources as part of the neoliberal, hegemonic ethos of "small government," for the more peripheral groups the IDF is likely to remain attractive for the symbolic rewards it can offer. Even labor immigrants (from Thailand and East Europe for example) may in the medium term acquire a selective entry ticket to the military as part of their naturalization process. Two simultaneous, contradictory processes – demilitarization and remilitarization – then, will affect the military's functioning.

With the rise of "identity politics," i.e., activity by culturally excluded groups aimed at reclaiming the acknowledgment of their distinctiveness, tensions are likely to become more acute in Israeli society as a whole, and in the military in particular, as different cultural groups compete for resources. This can be seen already in the accelerated promotion of women in the military in 2000, which led military and civilian rabbis to demand, successfully, that restrictions be imposed on the physical proximity of men and women in field units. Similarly, the flagrant presence of gays/lesbians in the IDF seeded homophobic trends from about 2005 onwards.

Summary

This chapter's point of departure was the need to get to the root of the fluctuations in the IDF's social status, which embodied a shift from the mythological "people's army" to an army plunged into a state of crisis with the civilian society, itself in a crisis of identity. Relations between the military and society in Israel have taken a cyclic course. Within a period of about twenty-five years, those relations have passed from the post-1967 climax of militarization to the demilitarization of the 1980s–1990s, and then back to remilitarization, as the conflict with the Palestinian Authority since 2000 indicates. Crucial to each phase was the social composition of the military, which determined the attitude of the groups within it to military service and to the burden entailed in waging a protracted war.

Militarization was driven by the rewards the Ashkenazi groups reaped from military service, central to which was their ability to translate their military dominance into legitimate social dominance owing to the army's role in defining the social hierarchy. When these rewards lost part of their value, with the burden of military sacrifice actually increasing rather than decreasing, what can be termed a "progressive motivation crisis" emerged. It was led by groups from the secular Ashkenazi middle class. At first the military way lost some of its legitimacy (especially after the First Lebanon War), as seen through the appearance of protest groups; later on, support for the allocation of material resources to the army declined (mid-1980s); and, finally, abandonment of the army was expressed in the various ways in which people distanced themselves from service (1990s).

The de-escalation of the Arab–Israeli conflict led, in the short term, to the Oslo Process and the withdrawal of militarism. In the long term it brought about the state's renewed ability to manage autonomous militaristic policies, largely because of the reconstruction of the army's social composition in favour of ethno-nationalist groups who displayed more loyalty to the military way. It was a gradual shift from the "people's army" to the "army of the peripheries." As the first years of the Al-Aqsa Intifada showed, the state regained much of its internal autonomy by reconstituting the equation between sacrifice and reward, this time by drawing on religious and peripheral groups. Nevertheless, the Israeli state shifted and modified its mode of warfare and initiated the partial withdrawal from the Palestinian-populated territories, starting with the "Disengagement Plan" from the Gaza Strip. Paradoxically, although the army gained more freedom of action as a result of the social realignment of its ranks, its resources were contracted by the market-oriented pressures. This worked to re-narrow its space of operation, especially when it comes to costly moves. Since the deemed fiasco in the Second Lebanon War has not reversed this trend, the decline of the IDF looks more certain than ever. The road to the volunteer-professional army is almost inevitable.

Cyclicality, which has typified Israel's history, is at a crossroads, now that the third cycle – remilitarization – has run its course. However, the cycle is neither endless nor one-directional. In Israel, at least, the relations between the new dominant groups of the future military and the dominant groups in society will determine the profile of the fourth cycle – back to the first or back to the second.

Further Reading

Arian, Asher 1995. *Security Threatened: Surveying Israeli Opinion on Peace and War.* New York: Cambridge University Press

Barnett, Michael N. 1992. *Confronting the Costs of War: Military Power, State, and Society in Egypt and Israel.* Princeton, NJ: Princeton University Press

Bar-Siman-Tov, Yaacov, et al. 2005. *The Israeli–Palestinian Violent Confrontation 2000–2004 – from Conflict Resolution to Conflict Management.* Jerusalem: Jerusalem Institute for Israel Studies

Barzilai, Gad 1996. *Wars, Internal Politics, and Political Order: a Jewish Democracy in the Middle East.* Albany, NY: State University of New York Press

Ben-Eliezer, Uri 1998. *The Making of Israeli Militarism.* Bloomington, IN: Indiana University Press

Ezrahi, Yaron 1997. *Rubber Bullets: Power and Conscience in Modern Israel.* Berkeley: University of California Press

Kimmerling, Baruch 2001. *The Invention and Decline of Israeliness: State, Society, and the Military*. Berkeley: University of California Press

Lomsky-Feder, Edna, and Ben-Ari Eyal (eds.) 1999. *The Military and Militarism in Israeli Society* Albany, NY: State University of New York Press

Maoz, Zeev 2006. *Defending the Holy Land: a Critical Analysis of Israel's Security and Foreign Policy*. Ann Arbor: University of Michigan Press

Peri, Yoram 2006. *Generals in the Cabinet Room: How the Military Shapes Israeli Policy*. Washington DC: United States Institute of Peace Press

Ram, Uri 2007. *The Globalization of Israel: McWorld in Tel Aviv, Jihad in Jerusalem*. London: Routledge

Swirski, Shlomo 2005. *The Price of Occupation: the Cost of the Occupation to Israeli Society*. Tel Aviv: Adva Center

6

The New Politics: Interest Groups and Alternative Channels

Shlomo Mizrahi

Previous chapters have described the central developments in Israeli society since the 1980s. In spite of the numerous conflicts, divisions, and tensions, both internaly and externally, Israeli society succeeds in keeping its democratic regime (at least formally), in making impressive economic and technological achievements, and in developing a rich cultural environment. Such success may seem an inherent paradox in Israeli society. Indeed, social scientists often argue that Israeli society, politics, and culture present us with an exceptional case as compared to other democratic regimes around the world and should, therefore, be analyzed using different methods. Without getting into the scientific debate, there is no doubt that there are some core characteristics that signify the "Israeli character" (and Israeli social and political culture) and allow Israeli society to overcome so many difficulties. In this chapter we try to trace these characteristics, suggesting that Israelis and Israeli society are noted for their entrepreneurship and independent initiatives, which together compose the vitality that makes Israeli society so dynamic and interesting. In some cases this entrepreneurship and these independent initiatives have led to failure but in most cases they have brought about changes in policy and institutions.

The "Israeli character" or habitus is expressed in all fields of life. In this chapter we will demonstrate how this entrepreneurship has enabled Israeli society to overcome deep divisions, fragmentation, and political inefficiency, leading to the evolution of new politics. Bringing together the discussion in previous chapters, we will show how deep social cleavages gradually led to a political stalemate and "nongovernability," so that Israeli citizens now face a reality in which they need to solve social problems on their own. This, together with a deeply rooted political culture, formed the grounds for the evolution of independent initiatives to provide governmental services in such a way that society gradually replaces the government. The evolution of this new style of politics could be regarded as a positive development in another context, yet in Israel it has been developed through illegal or semi-legal channels, thus reducing significantly the respect for law, and weakening democratic norms.

The nature of Israeli political culture and interest-group activity has been transformed in recent decades. In the first three decades after the establishment of the State of Israel in 1948, the economic, bureaucratic, and political systems were highly centralized and dominated by the Labor Party, which ruled the country between 1948 and 1977. Under these conditions the political culture was characterized by relatively passive attitudes on the part of citizens, and interest-group activity was very minor. The socio-political and economic processes since 1977 highlight the deep cleavages in Israeli society, which overloaded the political system and made it difficult to govern the country, leading to the evolution of the new politics. These cleavages, discussed in the first chapter, were described as the challenges to Israeli state and society and as underscoring the contemporary governance crisis. This chapter will demonstrate the political consequences of the fragmentation of Israeli society as political culture and activism change.

According to opinion polls, 30 percent of the Jewish-Israeli population regards the increased internal tension among various segments of the people as the most important problem on Israel's public agenda; 31 percent regards the slowdown in the economy as most important, while only 19 percent considers it to be the stalemate in the peace process. Since the polarizations in the various dimensions overlap, any Israeli government potentially faces significant domestic difficulties in building a consensus around policy strategies required in many areas.

The socio-economic dimension: Traditionally, the Israeli economy has been characterized as highly centralized owing to the socialist or state-controlled political culture (see chapter 4). The 1990s, however, have been characterized by privatization processes, with various social and economic consequences. These processes include market liberalization, deregulation, transfer of control and management to stockholders, and attempts by international companies to enter the Israeli market. Another aspect of these processes is the creation of flexibility and mobilization in the labor force, thus intensifying socio-economic inequality. Furthermore, security problems during the Palestinian uprising ("Intifada"), have made the Israeli economy dependent on cheap imported labor to replace cheap Palestinian workers. The numerous imported workers from Africa, South-East Asia, and Eastern Europe raise significant social, demographic, and moral problems as they suffer from very low wages, inequality, and a lack of basic social and labor rights. The growing socio-economic gaps together, with rising unemployment, have become one of the main issues dividing Israeli society, creating a potential for conflict. Furthermore, when the polarization of this dimension overlaps with polarization in other dimensions, the potential for conflict intensifies.

The ethnic–religious dimension: Israeli society is made up of Jewish immigrants from many countries. From the 1920s to the 1940s these immigrants came mainly from Europe, and created a predominantly Western-oriented culture. During the 1950s, after the establishment of the State of Israel, there was large-scale immigration from Arab and Muslim states, which changed the balance between the Western-oriented population segment, usually termed "Ashkenazim," and the Eastern-oriented population segment, usually termed "Mizrachim" or "Sephardim." The Mizrachim had difficulty in becoming established in a predominantly Western-oriented culture, with its discriminatory practices (see chapter 1). In the long term, this ethnic division merged with the socio-economic polarization: the lower classes were mostly composed of Mizrachim, and this intensified their feelings of discrimination and deprivation.

Furthermore, many Mizrachim were religiously observant, so an orthodox–secular division was added to the ethnic–religious and socio-economic divisions of Israeli society. On the other hand, national-religious Ashkenazim share the popular feeling of traditional Mizrachim against the liberal individualism, which they believe characterizes the willingness to negotiate with the Palestinians. In the current era of growing individualist ethos, religious Zionists are the sector most committed to the values of Israel's civil religion (for example, in military service; see chapter 5). The religious import of their political and cultural approach gives it a sense of holiness which separates religiously orthodox people from the rest of society. The combined polarization of the socio-economic and the ethnic–religious dimensions intensifies the conflicts between these population segments. It also makes it difficult to mobilize the entire society for a given cause, because the bonds that maintained a certain national consensus until 1977 no longer exist. The polarization in other dimensions further intensifies the problem.

The geographical dimension of center–periphery relations: Interestingly enough, polarization in the geographical dimension corresponds to the other aspects discussed thus far. Many new immigrants to Israel during the 1950s were sent to the peripheral regions, especially to development towns in the south and north of Israel, while the political, economic, and geographical centers (Tel Aviv and Jerusalem) were dominated by the upper- and middle-classe Ashkenazim (see chapter 1 and 2). As a result, the periphery is dominated by traditional and religious lower-class Mizrachim.

The security dimension relative to the Arab–Israeli conflict: This dimension has been dominant in Israeli society for most of the twentieth century (see chapter 1). The question of territorial compromise in exchange for peace has been at the center of political debate since the beginning of Zionism. Other questions, such as the nature of Jewish-Israeli identity, usually merged into this dimension. Until 1977 there was a national consensus on the policy adopted by the Labor-led government. However, the socio-political and economic processes discussed on pp. 95–8 also influenced this dimension. Since the early 1980s – and especially since the 1982 Israeli–Palestinian war in Lebanon – the polarization between right and left in Israeli society has intensified.

To a large extent this polarization fits the divisions in the other dimensions – lower-class voters, the Mizrachim, voters in the periphery, and religious voters traditionally support right-wing parties. Statistical analysis of electoral cleavages from 1969 to 1996, and an analysis of the 1996 election show that religious, Mizrachim, less educated, and lower status workers voted for the right-wing Likud and religious parties, whereas the left (Labor and Meretz) had a disproportionate share of secular, upper-class Ashkenazi voters. Since voting patterns significantly correlate with the preferences concerning the peace process, this cross-sectional characterization fits the polarization in the security dimension.

This argument is also supported by the findings of an ongoing monthly opinion poll by Ephraim Yuchtman-Yaar and Tamar

Hermann beginning in August 1993 and published under the title 'Peace Index' in *Haaretz* daily (www.tau.ac.il/peace/). These polls examined the public's attitudes toward the peace process in light of ongoing events and the divisions in Israeli society. According to this continuing opinion poll, the religious population in general, and the Ultra-Orthodox in particular, has assumed the role of the radical right-wing symbol for everything touching on the peace process. Among the Ultra-Orthodox only 20.5 percent support or greatly support the process; among those defining themselves as religious 43 percent support the process. On the other hand, 82 percent of traditionalist and 78 percent of secular groups declared their support for the process. Thus, low-class voters, Mizrachim, peripheral voters, and religious voters traditionally support right-wing parties. Although some of these voters do not completely accept the right-wing attitude to the Arab–Israeli conflict, they vote for right-wing parties because of their preferences in the other dimensions. As a result, Israeli society faces the paradox that a small majority of the population favors a territorial compromise, but this is not clearly expressed in the political division of power or in support for the actual negotiations with the Palestinians.

These deep cleavages forced the government to deal with increased, often contradictory, demands and made creating a consensus around any policy almost impossible. In particular, it has been difficult to implement the necessary reforms to the bureaucracy and the economy, which became stagnated by the late 1970s. The political and bureaucratic systems thus became significantly overloaded, resulting in a continuous failure of the government to provide services, and increased citizen dissatisfaction. Furthermore, many groups of society felt that traditional channels of democratic influence were effectively blocked and they attempted to find new ways to solve social problems. Indeed, since the 1980s Israeli society has undergone a significant transformation towards a new politics and changing relations between citizens and politicians. The roots of these transformations go back to the pre-statehood era.

The Origins of the New Politics

Israeli society and political culture were shaped under the British Administration in Palestine from 1917 to 1948. In these three decades, prior to the establishment of the State of Israel in 1948, the Jewish community in Israel had a relatively large measure of autonomy in managing its own affairs in most fields of life. The British Mandatory authorities enabled the Jewish (and Arab) communities to create a political party system based on a form of democratic election, to establish economic and industrial organizations, and to run autonomous systems of public health, social welfare, and education. For the Jewish community, this autonomy did not include the permission to freely settle the country, to have an independent military organization, or to enforce the rule of law toward the Jewish and the Arab population. The British policy of undermining independent initiatives of the Jewish community in these areas of life became very stringent in the 1930s and 1940s, owing to the intensifying conflict between the Jewish and Arab populations.

These structural conditions led the Jewish leadership to form a twofold strategy, which became the keystone of the Zionist ethos. First, whenever it was possible and authorized by the British Mandate, the Jewish leadership created independent organizations, alternative to those of either the British authorities or the Arab community, to accelerate economic development, provide public services, such as health, education, and welfare, and to develop infrastructure, such as electricity, roads, water supplies, and building construction. Thus, the idea that the Jewish community could not rely on others and had to create its own institutions and organizations gradually became a building block of the Zionist ethos. Second, the Jewish community faced significant threats from the Arab population and a British ban on wide Jewish immigration. In its aspiration to expand the Jewish settlement in Palestine as much as possible, the Jewish leadership gradually established illegal paramilitary forces that had three main goals: fighting the Arab paramilitary forces, organizing illegal Jewish immigration, and establishing and defending illegal settlements. These channels of activity became the bedrock of the Zionist ethos, as well as of the values that have been endowed, via the educational system, since the establishment of the State of Israel.

The process of Jewish institution-building in the pre-state period, which was, as noted, illegal in several important respects, had a significant influence on the political culture, belief system, and approach to conflict and problem solving in Israeli society after 1948. In other words, the ethos that was bequeathed to generations of Israelis included the idea that acting via unilateral initiatives on the margins of – or outside – the system of formal rules is not only permitted, but even serves national goals. To a large extent this was the modus operandi of Israeli society.

Prior to 1948 the Jewish institutional setting in Palestine, which was highly centralized, enabled politicians to repress similar initiatives directed toward the Jewish system itself. For the same reason, the approach of unilateral initiatives was repressed during the 1950s and 1960s, when Israel's political, administrative, and economic systems were highly centralized. The Labor Party, which led a coalition government during these decades, had a socialist orientation and therefore maintained a close involvement of the state and public administration in the economic system. Labor Party politicians also made use of political appointments. Party membership or inclination was considered a major criterion for entering the public sector in general and, in particular, for getting top positions in the civil service. The political system embodied a great deal of centralized and coherent governmental ability and did not hesitate to depress protest activities made by a few dissatisfied groups. This centralism prevented the development of strong interest groups and significantly slowed down the development of a civil society based on liberal values. During the 1950s and 1960s Israeli society did not exert significant pressure for change, even though political participation through voting was intense. Nevertheless, the approach of solving problems by unilateral initiatives was expressed during the 1950s and 1960s in two respects. First, the Labor-led political system implemented such an approach both towards citizens and in forming security and foreign policy. Citizens had little influence on public policy, which meant that policy was imposed from top down, and many decisions regarding the Arab–Israeli conflict, as well as defense and nuclear policy, were made without sufficient consideration of the attitudes of the international community or Israeli citizens. Second, at the level of personal relations, Israeli society developed informal routes to bypass the highly centralized bureaucracy, thereby partially implementing a "do-it-yourself" strategy. Since the centralized bureaucracy was inefficient, many Israelis used informal social networks to reach the person who could solve their problem. This strategy has been termed "protekzia," namely favoritism based on personal relations. Another strategy was turning to people who became experts in opening the closed channels of bureaucracy (termed "macher") and hiring them for bypassing the formal system.

The Evolution of Alternative Channels as New Politics

After the relative stability that characterized Israeli society during the 1950s and 1960s, a significant change in the development of Israeli political culture came in 1967 with the Six Day War (see chapter 3). It gave rise to nationalistic and religious feelings regarding the holy places in the West Bank. This change in the atmosphere was also expressed in attempts by religious people to establish illegal settlements in the West Bank and included the reappearance of the mode of behavior that had characterized the pre-state period, i.e., solving social problems through unilateral initiatives and disregarding existing formal rules. The first initiative was in Hebron in 1968, when a group of religious people decided to celebrate Passover in the old town of Hebron – a place that was settled by Jews until the 1929 Palestinian massacre and where the Tomb of the Patriarchs is considered a significant place for Jewish (and Muslim) worship. The Israeli military in charge in the occupied territories refused to authorize this event, but the group infiltrated the region illegally. After a negotiation process, a local agreement was reached stating that the celebration would be authorized but the group would leave the area immediately afterwards. The group has never left, and a settlement was established.

With the rise of nationalistic and religious feelings regarding the holy places in the West Bank, and the dissatisfaction of several religious sectors with the unwillingness of the Labor-led government to settle the territories, the creation of illegal settlements became the core activity of a large grassroots movement – Gush Emunim – the young guard of the mainstream Zionist National Religious Party. In their settlement activity during the 1970s they applied a strategy similar to that used by the Jewish leadership during the British Mandate – well-planned overnight forays. By the time the sun rose in the morning, several families were already living in temporary shelters, with the Israeli flag waving over their settlement. At first, there were several clashes with the government and the army, but in several instances the government actually gave up and cooperated with these illegal initiatives. Within a few years, the rules of the game regarding settlements in the occupied territories had changed, and with the rise of the right-wing Likud Party to power in 1977, settling the West Bank and Gaza Strip with Jewish settlements became formal policy. This led to a situation where over 200,000 Jewish-Israelis have settled in these territories, distributed in such a way that the situation is almost irreversible, with dire consequences for the Palestinians in the territories (see chapter 2) and resentment of pro-compromise Israelis.

This chain of events led to the evolution of alternative channels in many other fields of Israeli society, as dissatisfaction with the Israeli political system grew. The 1973 Yom Kippur War, when the Israeli army was caught by surprise, triggered strong criticism against the Labor-led government. This dissatisfaction was revealed in the the 1977 elections, when the Labor Party lost its dominant position after twenty-nine years of leading the country. The right-wing Likud Party formed a coalition government but was unable to repeat the dominance of the Labor Party or to recreate the consensus (see chapter 3). The developments in the 1970s unveiled the deep fragmentation and divisions in Israeli society, which also found expression in the evolution of mass movements – notably, Peace Now and Gush Emunim, which expressed the left-wing and right-wing positions, respectively, regarding the Arab–Israeli conflict.

To change the ruling coalition and its policy, the Israeli public used legal, democratic channels such as elections, demonstrations, strikes, and the mass media. During the 1970s the political system therefore remained relatively non-fragmented; the economic and bureaucratic systems were highly centralized and public dissatisfaction was expressed mainly through regular forms of political participation such as protests, demonstrations, and interest-group activity. The forms of political participation changed significantly in the 1980s, when demographic and structural social changes that had begun in the 1970s deepened (see chapters 1 and 3). Since the Likud and Labor parties constituted two political blocs which had almost equal power in the parliament, religious parties that had a loyal constituency had a pivotal position between the two blocs. The influence of the religious political parties, and particularly that of Ultra-Orthodox parties, grew, and the status of religion in public life became stronger. Religious parties gradually raised their demands in the coalition negotiations and the result was increased dominance of religion in public life and what was perceived by secularists as growing benefits to the Ultra-Orthodox, especially the extension of exemption from military service. Secular Jews thus felt that religious norms were enforced on them without their being able to change anything, as the religious would hold power in any coalition formed. Political life was characterized by a continuous degeneration of the main systems of the political parties and their leaderships. Furthermore, the political wheeling and dealing between the coalition parties continued, and the level of the political debate declined drastically.

The political system was transformed into a fragmented, overloaded, system, characterized by an increasing number of parties and great difficulty in creating viable coalitions. These dynamics created the impression among the public that the government could not produce stable policy decisions, largely because the bureaucratic and economic systems remained highly centralized and because disagreements were so strong. The unstable situation – high inflation and the war in Lebanon – and the election results led the Likud Party and the Labor Party to form a national unity government in 1984, agreeing on an economic plan and a partial withdrawal from Lebanon. However, they could not reach agreement on many other issues, and so this government and its successor in 1988 entered a political stalemate.

The inability of the government to make efficient and stable policy decisions, as well as the political stalemate, intensified dissatisfaction among the Israeli public with the government's provision of public services and created the feeling that the channels to influence government and public life were effectively blocked. Nevertheless, the majority of the population complied with the spirit of the formal, democratic rules, even though it regarded the fragmented social structure and the inefficiency of politicians and public administrators as the source of the problem. The crisis went even deeper than a systemic governmental inability to provide services, because there were no other agreed social mechanisms for compromise and for solving conflicts between sectors and groups in society.

The deep social fragmentation reflected the inability of social groups to find agreed ways or informal rules to solve social problems. During the 1980s, large sectors of Israeli society attempted to find alternative means of solving social problems or achieving personal desires and social aims. These sectors – in a similar way to the settlers (see pp. 153) – interpreted the problem of government failure combined with blocked influence channels as an "old problem." Groups and individuals therefore often took action against the law with the belief that "there is no other way." As a result, the 1980s were characterized by a significant growth in the "black-market economy" – particularly regarding illegal trade in foreign currency, "gray-market medicine" – expressed in a semi-legal private supply of health services using public facilities, "gray-market education" – expressed in the occupation of privately paid teachers and the evolution of independent private schools, and pirate cable television networks – all of which are an alternative provision of governmental services.

Indeed, during the 1980s it became clear that, for many people, only unilateral and at times illegal initiatives could help improve their outcomes. Most of these initiatives were finally institutionalized via the formal rules of the game and became part of governmental policy. Decentralization increased in the fields of foreign currency trade and the communications market. In the fields of education and health care, the government changed the rules in the direction signaled by society and initiated several reform plans towards decentralization. These processes had a direct impact on specific policies and outcomes, and in the 1990s, Israeli economic and administrative systems became more decentralized than in the previous decades (see chapter 4).

However, these processes addressed only specific problems of public service provision; the fundamental structural problems and inefficiencies of the Israeli political system remained unchanged or even intensified. This situation gave rise to the second stage of the learning process and the spreading and deepening of alternative channels of new politics. In effect, that meant that the conditions which had motivated the previous processes continued to exist in the 1990s. Each time citizens employ the strategy of unilateral initiatives, they internalize it as the main way of problem solving in any dimension and on any matter, so people gradually learned that compromise and bargaining were inferior to unilateral initiatives and non-compromising positions as mechanisms for solving problems. As a result, since the 1990s there have been deep behavioral changes in Israeli society, towards lack of tolerance, increased violence, and increased social alienation and fragmentation. For example, a cross-cultural study shows a significant decline in the level of tolerance towards minorities among Israelis, disrespect for human rights, deep social cleavages, and a decline in public support for democratic norms and for the rule of law.[1] Trust in hierarchical organizations such as the Israeli army and the Supreme Court has been relatively high throughout the years, although even this has changed lately.

In the 1990s Israeli citizens made extensive use of unilateral initiatives and alternative politics in a wide variety of fields. For example, in the field of internal security, the feeling of many Israelis that the police did not provide sufficient security triggered the evolution of

---

[1]   Asher Arian, David Nachmias, Doron Navot, and Daniel Shani, *Israel Democracy Index* (2003–6, published yearly). Jerusalem: The Israeli Democracy Institute. (In Hebrew.)

privately paid security services, protecting against crime and theft in many neighborhoods and small towns. In the field of social welfare, as a result of the growth in socio-economic gaps and the failure of the government to provide sufficient support for the poor, Israeli society has witnessed tremendous growth in the number of voluntary organizations for helping weaker groups of society, in terms of both financial support and consultation. In 1980 the Knesset legislated the NGOs law, which simplified the registration process of new NGOs. Since then approximately 30,000 new NGOs have been registered (an average of 1600 per year). Although not all of them are active, this impressive growth signifies retrenchment of the welfare state and a move towards alternative politics in the welfare services. In recent years non-profit organizations have significantly increased their share in social and economic interactions and as a result their impact on political decision-making has been strengthened as well.

In the field of church–state relations, many Israelis, who felt uncomfortable with the Israeli religious authorities' monopoly of marriage and divorce procedures, have taken the unilateral initiative of civil marriage outside Israel – especially in Cyprus. Israeli authorities and courts have had no choice but to recognize these marriages because of international agreements. The problem widened as many of the newcomers from the FSU not recognized as Jewish by the rabbinate could not marry in Israel. While the political system was unable to reach a decision on marriage reform, unilateral initiatives were the solution. In this manner, citizens' unorganized activity actually created the start of a separation between religion and state in a very important respect.

Another central field where Israelis adopted unilateral initiatives that led to the formation of informal norms concerns military service – both in the regular and in the reserve forces. In Israel, every citizen reaching the age of eighteen must join the army by the rule of law. Men have to serve for three years and women for two years. They are paid a symbolic salary, meaning that they are actually obliged to volunteer to serve in the army. After they are released from duty, most Israeli men, and to a limited extent also women, have to serve in the reserve forces – approximately one month per year for 20–30 years. For several decades, the deep militarization of Israeli society ensured that most people would serve in the army and relatively few have used the available justifications for not serving, e.g., religious reasons (especially for women), conscientious objection, or mental or physical disability. However, during the 1980s, and increasingly during

the 1990s, socio-cultural processes of increased individualization and
a decline of the national-military ethos significantly weakened the
motivation to serve in the army. Although similar processes happened
in other Western countries, in Israel this phenomenon is termed "the
motivation crisis." Many potential soldiers have used the justifications
provided by the law to pull out of service – in both the regular and
the reserve forces. During the 1990s there was a significant increase
in the number of citizens who avoided service for reasons related to
religion, mental and physical health, and conscientious objections such
as pacifism.

The important point is that Israeli citizens did not become more religious or more ill during the 1990s, but simply enjoyed the cooperation
of authorized persons, both inside and outside the army, to enable them
to withdraw from service. This resulted in a significant decline in the
percentage of citizens who served in the regular and reserve forces.
These trends have been gradually recognized by the army, which
has initiated several reform programs planned to institutionalize the
new situation, by dropping the voluntary aspect and emphasizing the
material incentives of military service. This is likely to affect the socio-
economic profile of the army and is expected to lead to policy shifts,
both within the army itself and in the political system – shifts that have
already started to appear and are discussed in chapter 5.

The emergence of new politics embodies an even deeper change
in the nature of relations between citizens and politicians in Israel. In
the 1950s and 1960s, these relations were informally based on a top-
down approach, in the sense that policies were decided through the
highly centralized system with very limited participation of citizens.
In the 1980s and 1990s the nature of these informal relations has been
transformed, and they have been based on a bottom-up approach. In
this new informal status quo, citizens identify policy problems and
solve them unilaterally, by forming substitutive services. In doing so,
they actually signal the required institutional change to politicians and
thus institutional changes as well as specific policies and outcomes are
initiated from the bottom up.

The Supreme Court as a Channel of Political Participation

The high magnitude of alternative channels in Israeli society inspired
many citizens to look for alternative centers of power. In Israel this

alternative center of power has been to a large extent the High Court of Justice (HCJ), which, by the late 1990s, had become a partial substitute for the political system, which was unable to perform for the reasons described above. The fragmented political system was unable to mediate between contending group claims and to provide answers for individuals and minority groups seeking justice. Thus, issues of citizenship and naturalization, marriage and divorce, or demands for equal treatment were brought to the Court as a measure of last resort.

Historically, in the absence of a written constitution, the HCJ had significantly limited its involvement in social and political issues by demanding petitioners to show a clear interest in the case ("standing" in legal terms) and thus refused to hear the vast majority of the petitions filed to the Court in the 1950s and 1960s. This situation started to change in the late 1970s, when the HCJ gradually opened its gates and showed a willingness to hear almost any kind of petition without questioning too much standing and justiciability. This process was accelerated in the late 1980s and early 1990s, when the political left wing was driven to the HCJ by the feeling that it lacked the ability to bear any political influence. Having understood the nature of the Court's decisions and being aware that in certain matters other politicians would not object, left-wing politicians increased the frequency of their petitions to the High Court of Justice, thus advancing their own and their party's interests.

By turning to the Court, these politicians, who could alternatively advance changes to formal institutions through the formal parliamentary legislative process, actually adopted an approach of unilateral initiative that they found more rewarding than the stagnant political system. Although these, and other, politicians were seeking to advance their own interests, as argued by researchers such as Hofnung, Dotan, and Benvenisti, their political strategy gained legitimacy from a wider political culture of alternative politics. In an atmosphere where anything goes and everyone seeks (semi-legal) ways to establish a *fait accompli*, the HCJ was regarded as an alternative, legitimate channel for achieving desired ends. The HCJ benefited from the fact that politicians sought its authority, and established its status among the policymakers.

In an environment where all players engaged in unilateral initiatives and alternative politics, the Court actually joined in and set its own borders of authority: it also adopted an approach of unilateral initiative, informally positioning itself as the "rights defender." Yet, while this was true for justifiability and standing (the permission to appeal to the

Court regarding the interest of the general public), when referring to
judicial activism in the Court's ruling, the rate of judicial intervention
in security, social rights, and religious issues was relatively limited.
In the petition of *Ressler* v. *The Minister of Defense to the HCJ*, the
Court was asked to change the decision of the Minister of Defense to
exempt Ultra-Orthodox people from military service. This exemption
in itself is another example of the political system's difficulties. What
began as a temporary and limited exemption in 1948 has widened
without proper legislation, and every year the minister of defense uses
his authority to postpone the conscription of yeshiva students. Secular activists demanded that the government end this exemption and,
unable to influence the government (because of the political power
of the Ultra-Orthodox), appealed to the Court. Justice Aharon Barak,
however, determined that: "In every case, there is the law, and in every
case, there are the varying degrees within the law." Yet, although the
case was heard by the Court, the ruling was that the decision of the
minister of defense was reasonable, and therefore was not changed.
Only in the late 1990s did the Court order the government to legislate
the rules of exemption properly, which by 2006 it had not yet done.

Frustration with the parliamentary system brought not only politicians but also many groups in Israeli society to turn to the Court in
the late 1980s, and increasingly in the 1990s, to defend their interests. These groups included, for example, gays, left- and right-wing
parties, and parliamentarians, professional groups such as the Israel
Investment Managers' Office, Women's Lobby, writers and journalists, Israeli-Arabs, non-Israeli Arabs, students, Ultra-Orthodox Jews,
and secular Jews. All these petitions transformed the Supreme Court
into a central player in the policymaking process thus also increasing
the political aspects of its activity.

These characteristics of the new politics became even more evident
towards the late 1990s. Gradually, it became clear that almost any decision made by the government or parliament was likely to be brought to
the HCJ by a certain dissatisfied group. As a result, politicians started to
consider the possible attitudes and positions of the HCJ in any policymaking process. This has been expressed, for example, in an informal
conduct rooted in the Knesset (Israeli parliament), through its legal
adviser, who activates a system that checks the compatibility of any
draft law to the basic laws, in order to avoid Court intervention. In
this manner, the Knesset avoids legislation that contradicts the basic
laws and actually adopts an approach of restrained legislation. Such an

approach was seen, for example, in the draft laws regarding land agents (1992), the Trans-Israel Highway (1994), investment advisors (1995), and motor vehicle insurance (1996).

In effect, any government decision is potentially subjected to the Court's criticism and politicians therefore attempt to interpret the Court's attitudes towards their decisions and construct policies that can be defended in Court. This informal conduct, which places the Court as an almost complete substitute for the government, was clearly evident in the decisions regarding the location of the fence built by the Israeli government to divide the Jewish and Arab populations in the occupied territories. Virtually all political decisions on this matter have been brought to the Court by various petitioners, and the Court's decisions have been final. Hundreds of kilometers of the fence which had already been built were relocated as the result of Court decisions. This has also encouraged a hot debate among Israeli politicians, academics, lawyers, and the public regarding the need for a constitutional court that would have the authority to invalidate the parliament's rules and would represent the various factions of Israeli society.

The New Politics and the Policy towards the Israeli–Palestinian Conflict

As explained earlier, the political discourse in Israel is dominated by the developments in the Israeli–Palestinian conflict. To a large extent, this conflict is reflected in many aspects of policy decisions and political culture. At the same time, Israeli political culture is characterized by alternative politics. Interestingly enough, this mode of political culture became so dominant in Israeli society that it is strongly reflected in the strategies of the Israeli public and politicians towards the Israeli–Palestinian conflict. This assimilation expresses the high magnitude of alternative politics in Israeli society.

In the summer of 2002 the Likud government, headed by Ariel Sharon, decided on the construction of a separation fence between Israel and the Palestinian territories. The election of Sharon after the collapse of the Camp David talks was a result of a growing consensus among Israelis on the "no partner" thesis offered by Barak after Camp David. Although the Likud was elected because of its hard-line approach towards Palestinians, it did not take long to realize that the military campaign was at most only partially able to bring security. The right-wing Likud previously objected to the idea of the fence, raised by the Labor Party and other dovish factions, as it was concerned that the fence, built for security purposes, would eventually draw the border between Israel and the Palestinians. But, the growing numbers of Israeli casualties from suicide bombers who infiltrated from the West Bank into Israel and the growing public pressure for security have caused the government to support the construction of the fence.

The fence was a unique strategy in two important and interrelated measures. First, in the wake of Camp David and the following cycle of violence a large number of Israelis became weary of the peace process but, especially as violence escalated, were interested in separation as a security measure. Second, the decision to build a fence was very much a bottom-up process influenced by citizens' organized demands and local initiatives, which ignored Palestinian demands and interests. The empowerment of domestic politics focused on a short-term, immediate solution.

Between 1994 and 2002 different initiatives along the seam line created new facts. The residents of the Gilboa regional council decided to begin to build a 12-kilometer fence against infiltrations of Palestinian terrorists. The regional council mayor, Dani Atar, traveled to the USA to raise funds for the construction of the fence. "This is a message to the government," explained the mayor, "there is total anarchy and disregard for the personal security of citizens."[2] Another regional mayor explained: "I have to take care of the security of my residents. They [policymakers] can call it a security fence or an agricultural fence . . . if policymakers would call it separation it would appear as withdrawal, so they use security terms."[3] Atar predicted that if the security situation worsened, policymakers would have to adapt accordingly and gradually the border would become a reality. Furthermore, as the building of the fence proceeded in 2003 and 2004, the Israeli public as well as the Palestinian population appealed to the High Court of Justice, as a substitute for the formal political system, regarding the exact path of the fence.

The more terrorism has taken its toll, the more various groups that advocated the fence have raised their voice, demanding that the government provide the necessary funding. The "Fence for Life" movement, established in 2001, initiated a large campaign that demanded the construction of the fence to prevent the infiltration of suicide

---

[2] *Haaretz* daily, December 15, 2002.   [3] *Haaretz* daily, December 17, 2002.

bombers, regardless of the withdrawal or the future of the settlements. Israel's President, Moshe Katzav, who met with the leaders of the group, expressed his support for a security fence. The "fence for life" campaign attempted to circumvent the political debate by deliberately avoiding the discussion of withdrawal or stating a position regarding the future of the territories. This position enabled the movement to receive support from politicians of various parties. Uzi Dayan, a retired major general and the head of the "Forum for National Responsibility," a dovish movement that includes many former generals, described the fence as a security measure with long-term significance for the preservation of Israel as a Jewish and democratic state against the "demographic threat."

The fence, therefore, was not only a short-term security measure, but according to some of its proponents also a part of a wider strategy that would eventually create peace by reducing friction and restoring confidence among Israelis. Disengagement was adopted by part of Israel's peace supporters, who believed that the idea of separation from the Palestinians, using the vantage point of Israeli interest could mobilize large parts of Israeli society to support an end to the occupation. The "Council for Peace and Security," a voluntary organization made up of retired military personnel with dovish views, explained that since the political process had reached a dead end, Israel should move towards unilateral separation. Separation would ease the strain on the security budget, enhance Israel's defense capabilities, narrow the friction points with the Palestinians, reduce the danger of regional escalation, and contain the "negative" demographic process in which Jews are becoming a minority between the Jordan and the sea. In the long run, this partition could be the base for a renewed peace process.

The Labor Party's attempt to use the idea of unilateral separation in the 2002 election has failed to make the difference. But with the growing cycles of suicide violence largely immune to Israel's defense measures, the idea received a life of its own. Surveys indicate that a majority of Israelis (83 percent) supports a unilateral disengagement, even at the price of evacuation of (some) settlements, and believes that the fence can prevent or significantly reduce terrorism.

In the summer of 2002, under public pressure, the Likud government began the construction of a fence between the territories and Israel. Ariel Sharon, who had previously objected to the fence, had, according to his senior adviser and campaign manager, Eyal Arad, to adopt the idea: "there was a situation that the prime minister was blamed for any terrorist attack . . . what caused the change was the pressure of public opinion."[4] The building of the fence was interrupted by budgetary questions, the protests of Israeli settlers, who opposed a fence that would leave some of them outside and demanded that the fence be extended eastward, and the American government's demands that the fence not annex territories. In spite of all the difficulties, the construction of the fence proceeded and by 2005 a large part of the project was completed.

The campaign for the fence was paralleled by a campaign for unilateral withdrawal or disengagement from Gaza and parts of the West Bank. While the "fence for life" campaign avoided the discussion of withdrawal, or even advocated the protection of secluded settlements, with the forces the fence would free, other campaigns advocated a gradual withdrawal and the removal of settlements. The Disengagement Plan adopted by Sharon was the logical continuation of the fence strategy, in the reduction of friction points between Israelis and Palestinians and in withdrawing from a densely populated area to which most Israelis were unattached. Like the fence, this idea was the result of the growing belief that "there is no partner" on the other side and that, consequently, Israel should redeploy its forces according to its own interests. Like the fence, this initiative was supported by many on the left, but also by the center and moderate right who believed that the price of holding Gaza, or the withdrawal from Gaza, would allow Sharon to hold important parts of the West Bank. More important, the unilateral withdrawal plan, unlike the fence, also received support from abroad. In his own party, Sharon's plan to remove all settlements from Gaza and about four settlements from the West Bank was heavily criticized, but it was warmly embraced by the US government and President Bush congratulated Sharon on his initiative. Therefore, on June 6, 2004 the Israeli government accepted the Disengagement Plan, which included the removal of all settlements in Gaza, to be completed by the end of 2005.

Although it was not directly imposed on the government by unilateral initiatives, the strategy of unilateral disengagement was clearly influenced by them. Instead of negotiation and compromise, the Israeli political culture adopts methods of unilateralism, often with disregard for others and for the long-term effects. This shows how deeply

---

[4]   *Ynet*, August 4, 2003.

alternative politics have been assimilated into all levels and aspects of Israeli politics.

The New Politics and Human Rights Organizations

Violations of human rights in democratic systems are usually case-related rather than an openly stated and consistent policy. This is also the situation in Israel, where governmental authorities are obliged to fulfill the individual fundamental "natural" rights and the Israeli Knesset is obliged to fulfill fundamental rights stated in the Basic Laws of 1992, that is, Basic Law: Human Dignity and Liberty and Basic Law: Freedom of occupation. As a consequence, human rights organizations usually adopt a case-related strategy by which they assist people in specific cases to defend their rights, rather than attempting to lead attitudinal changes in society in support of human rights or to take the political-constitutional route. This is also the reason why these organizations regard the Court as their natural, if not only, ally in defending human rights and helping people in litigation.

Human rights activists and NGOs in Israeli society play a central role in empowering the Supreme Court as a political player and human rights defender. For example, the public struggle of Shatil, established by the New Israel Fund, to add sixty-one new pre-compulsory kindergartens in the academic year 2000/1 and to open the first library to serve the Bedouin population in the Negev was focused on legal channels. In a similar vein, following the petition filed by Bizchut, the Israel Human Rights Center for People with Disabilities, the High Court of Justice ordered an examination of over two hundred new buses, to assess their accessibility for people in wheelchairs.

Likewise, following the petition filed by the Association for Civil Rights in Israel (ACRI), the High Court of Justice ordered termination, within two months, of the acceptance proceedings of the Arab Ka'adan family to the Jewish settlement of Katzir. This settlement, like many others, had an acceptance proceeding and the Ka'adan family argued that they fulfilled all the requirements but were rejected because of their Arab identity. In 1995, the High Court of Justice, accepting a petition filed by ACRI, ordered the revocation of Rule 27 of the Rules of the Israel Bar Association, which had enabled attorneys to retain a client's case files, thus preventing the client from going to another attorney. Similarly, in 1996, another ACRI petition, concerning discrimination in the registration of Arab children to kindergartens in Jaffa, came to a successful end. Under pressure from the High Court of Justice, the criteria were revised for accepting children to kindergartens, and the practice of discrimination was eliminated. Thus, while laws often remain unchanged, human right activists are able to score victories in "local" battles in the courts. These rulings, however, have often turned the court itself into a target of criticism by right-wing or religious activists and, consequently, undermined its status in Israeli society.

Another central channel of human rights activities concerns military behavior in the West Bank. Here, again, the failure to resolve the central issue of the occupation has led human rights activists to take more limited initiatives to help Palestinians with everyday life. These activities are also influenced by the emergence of the new politics, as can be seen in the operation of Machsom Watch (checkpoint watch), a civil rights movement, consisting exclusively of women, founded in 2001. The media reports about human rights abuses of Palestinians at the many checkpoints the IDF set up throughout the West Bank allegedly to perform security checks on the Palestinian population, stimulated several activists to establish the initiative. Machsom Watch monitors the behavior of soldiers and police at checkpoints through which Palestinians enter Israel, to ensure that the human and civil rights of Palestinians are protected and to report the results of the observations. Four hundred Jewish women are voluntarily active in the organization, most of whom are middle-class, professional women. In practice, every day the organization's activists stand by each of the main checkpoints and watch how Palestinian civilians are treated by the soldiers. Perceived patterns of abuse and humiliation are documented and reported and very often the activists intervene on site, and even help Palestinians in their interaction with soldiers. Symbolically, as Machsom Watch activists state, their "quiet but assertive, presence at checkpoints is a direct challenge to the dominant militaristic discourse that prevails in Israeli society."[5] Indeed, women watchers have often clashed with their "watched" men.

The activities were criticized by left-wing activists, who advocate struggling against occupation rather that ameliorating its effects. This seems to be a major dilemma of Israeli NGOs, who debate between changing the system or providing assistance. Thus, organizations

---

[5]   Machsom Watch, www.machsomwatch.org/eng/aboutUsEng&lang=eng (May 30, 2006).

established to help the poor through distribution of food and clothing are criticized for perpetuating inequality and, unintentionally, supporting neoliberalism by relieving the government of its duties for its citizens. Under the existing political stalemate, human rights and other civic organizations are discouraged from pursuing political change and encouraged to concentrate on local initiatives instead.

Summary

The independence, initiative, and entrepreneurship which are so typical of the Israeli character have been responsible for many of Israel's failings since 1980, but these same characteristics have also enabled the Israelis to overcome the deep divisions, fragmentation, and political inefficiency of their state, and to put forward a more optimistic vision of the future of Israeli society.

Since the 1980s Israeli society has adopted a special mode of political behavior – providing public services such as health, education, internal security, media channels, and welfare via non-institutionalized channels as an alternative to those of the government, and often illegally. The 1980s were characterized by a significant growth in the "black-market economy" – particularly regarding illegal trade in foreign currency, "gray-market medicine" – reflected in a semi-legal private supply of health services using public facilities, "gray-market education" – expressed in the employment of privately paid teachers and the evolution of independent private schools, and pirate cable networks – all of which are alternative provision of governmental services. In the 1990s, this mode of behavior spread to other policy areas such as internal security, social welfare, human rights activities, and even the policy towards the Arab–Israeli conflict. Indeed, during the 1990s it became clear that almost only initiatives of this kind could help people improve their situation. The Supreme Court has become a central channel of political participation, serving also as a channel for citizens to express their dissatisfaction with the government decisions or lack of decisions. The Israeli government responded positively to those initiatives by changing policy in the direction demanded by those groups. In the long run, this mode of behavior led to significant policy and institutional changes towards reduced governmental provision of public services and transformed the nature of relations between citizens and politicians from a top-down orientation into a much more complex composition, where citizens provide services on their own, thus forcing the government to institutionalize certain mechanisms.

Further Reading

Arian, Asher. 1997. *The Second Republic – Politics in Israel*. Chatham, NJ: Chatham House

Barzilai, Gad 1996. *Wars, Internal Conflicts and Political Order: a Jewish Democracy in the Middle East*. New York: State University of New York Press

Horowitz, Dan, and Moshe Lissak 1978. *Origins of the Israeli Polity: Palestine under the Mandate*. Chicago: Chicago University Press

Horowitz, Dan, and Moshe Lissak 1989. *Trouble in Utopia: the Overburdened Polity of Israel*. Albany: State University of New York Press

Lehman–Wilzig, Samuel N. 1992. *Wildfire: Grassroots Revolts in Israel in the Post-Socialist Era*. Albany: State University of New York Press

Conclusion: the State of the State

Guy Ben-Porat

Since 1980 Israel has turned into a multicultural state. This is neither a normative statement nor a description of a constitutional design as in other multicultural states that have committed themselves to inclusion and equality. Rather, the reality of Israel's multiculturalism is a large national minority, persisting ethnic identities, and recent immigrations, which contest the existing social order and public institutions. Multiculturalism in Israel, consequently, is not an end point but rather a novel reality, yet to be fully recognized, in which a consensus based on uniformity is unlikely in the near future, so new social arrangements and political agreements, and modes of cooperation between different groups must be sought for the sake of state, society, and democracy. This is especially pertinent as intensifying social cleavages – national, ethnic, religious, ideological, and socio-economic – undermine social solidarity, overburden the political system, and impede the functioning of Israeli democracy to the dangerous point of "ungovernability."

Israeli democracy is endangered by the growing schisms between groups and by the state's inability to govern – that is to provide long-term acceptable solutions for the mounting dilemmas and to rule everyday life effectively. Deep schisms force the government to deal with increased, often contradictory, demands, and creating a consensus around any policy is almost impossible. This has resulted in overburdening and a governance crisis that is reflected in the difficulty of making decisions and, consequently, in the declining trust of citizens in state institutions and in other groups in society. Surveys conducted by the Israel Democracy Institute find an overall support for democracy but a declining trust in state institutions, growing dissatisfaction with government policy and the ability to maintain the rule of law, and, most significantly, growing alienation from politicians and political parties. This alienation explains the decline in the turnout at the last elections, held in 2006. Relations between groups in society are also perceived as negative by citizens, according to the 2006 survey and in the survey held in 2005, ten years after Rabin's assassination, more than 80 percent of respondents believed that a political assassination could happen again.[1] Israeli groups are segregating behind real or imagined walls that separate religious from secular, Arab from Jew, and rich from poor.

Beyond the formal support for democracy there are aspects relating to the core democratic values of equality and tolerance that cause concern. While 85 percent of the population believes that Israel should be a democracy, 62 percent believes that the government should encourage Arabs to emigrate from Israel. Scholars have described Israel as a "non-liberal democracy," which in contrast to the liberal democracy, whose first priority is the individual and his/her rights, puts a strong emphasis on the collective or community. This illiberal character of Israeli democracy has significant consequences for the status of minorities and especially to the Arab citizens of the states. Intolerance towards Arabs is especially high but intolerance between religious and secular groups and, to a lesser degree, between ethnic groups is also high. The result, is twofold: growing segregation and alienation between sectors and, consequently, decline of trust and alienation from the political system.

The governance crisis, therefore, is expressed in low levels of trust, political instability, growing tensions between groups, contradictory demands from government and its institutions, and the erosion of the rule of law described in the previous chapter. This crisis has led to attempts at political and constitutional reform, with limited success so far. Political reforms suggested pertain mostly to political instability and the need to strengthen the elected government by reducing the number of political parties, granting more power to the prime minister or, in the most recent campaign, to implement a presidential regime. The suggested "technical" reforms may provide some stability to the system at the expense of representation, so would satisfy some groups but alienate others. The important point, as the previous chapters have demonstrated, is that instability is probably an effect rather than a cause – the result of the growing schisms within society.

---

[1] See all surveys on the Israel Democracy Institute website: www.idi.org.il.

The initiative to write a constitution for Israel seems to engage exactly with these issues, as both the work done in the Knesset Constitution, Law, and Justice Committee and the latest, much publicized, campaign of the Democracy Institute seek to find agreement through negotiations between the different contesting groups. The constitution is designed not only to fill a supposed vacuum in Israel and to provide required protection for citizen's rights, but also to underscore agreements that would be reached between the different groups in Israeli society. These (dis)agreements, however, are exactly what could prevent the making of a meaningful constitution. Differently stated, a constitution that would provide solutions for the contemporary dilemmas would be dependent upon the ability to resolve the very tensions that threaten the democratic regime. Let us summarize the dilemmas presented throughout this book.

Land for Peace? The Borders of the State

The territorial dilemma that has occupied Israeli politics since 1980 is likely to continue in forthcoming years. The settlement project in the West Bank that took off in this period created facts on the ground that would make any settlement difficult, as resistance to any removal of settlements is more than likely. The growing costs of the occupation, which have been revealed since the Palestinian resistance began to make its mark in 1987, led to an attempt in 1993 to resolve the conflict, which failed because Israel was reluctant to withdraw to the green line and Palestinian Authority was reluctant to accept any less than that withdrawal. The collapse of the peace process revealed not only the difference in expectations between the sides, but also the lack of trust, which has grown since then with the Palestinian election of the Hamas government. Unilateral attempts by Israel to determine its borders caused frustrations among Palestinians and exposed the deep schism within Israeli society.

The future of the territories is the main political dividing line in Israel, and the right–left schism is exposed each time a withdrawal is discussed or implemented. The question of the territories is not only a matter of security but also of identity and touches the exposed nerves of Israeli society. The assassination of Rabin in 1995 was the peak of political violence, but the withdrawal from Gaza and the removal of settlements highlighted the rift that even today prevents the government from implementing decisions to remove Jewish illegal settlements in the West Bank.

The question of the future borders is a complex one that involves, on the one hand, the political and other rights of the Palestinians and, on the other hand, the future political, economic, and legal structure of Israel. During the 1990s, and again in 2005, it seemed that partition was all but inevitable as even the right-wing Likud came to this conclusion. The pendulum swings of the peace process, however, have proved that details matter, as both the internal debate and the external negotiations revealed repeatedly. "Only after the internal Israeli territorial debate comes to an end," the conclusion of chapter 3 states, "will the political and governmental system be able to stabilize according to the new coordinates." Yet, it is safe to assume this will be the prelude to no less interesting internal debates over Israel's dual commitment – Jewish and democratic – which raises another set of dilemmas, both related to and independent from the question of its external boundaries. It is not only the question of how to balance "Jewish" and "democratic," and whether the two contradict, but also what each of these definitions means in itself.

Jewish and Democratic – What Does Democracy Mean?

If a democracy is measured by its tolerance of minorities and protection of minority rights, the Arab minority is an important test case for Israel's democratic regime. The chapters of this book have described the inferior status of the Arab minority in the job market, land allocation, immigration policy, and resource distribution. The amelioration of these problems, besides attending to specific needs and discriminations, raises more structural questions regarding the future of the state.

Hopes placed on the peace process during the 1990s were short-lived, and not only because the difficulties of the process, and its eventual collapse, brought to the fore, once again, dilemmas of loyalty and identity. The emphasis on partition and the promise that it would ensure the future of the Jewish state were not matched with a discussion of the status of the Arab minority. Moreover, the collapse of the peace process and the deep internal (Jewish) cleavages exposed in the assassination of Prime Minister Rabin caused Jewish society to turn inwards for security and reconciliation. Arab and Jewish citizens drew apart from each other, became more suspicious, and the political discourse has grown negative, if not hostile.

Minority rights can be achieved in two possible ways – either by liberal equality in a "color-blind society," which ignores differences and prevents discrimination, or by group rights, which grant autonomy and status to ethnic and national groups. Each approach has more merits and shortcomings than we are able to discuss here, and each approach raises more questions regarding public and private, groups and the state, equality and special treatment and the democratic procedures. This discussion between the Jewish majority and the Arab minority is yet to begin.

Jewish and Democratic – What Is a Jewish State?

Paradoxically, the vast majority of Jewish Israelis strongly agree that Israel is a Jewish state, but strongly disagree over what a Jewish state means. The source of disagreement is largely the role of religion in public life. Previous arrangements known as the "status quo" that managed the differences are being eroded by demographic, economic, and political changes and new agreements are difficult to reach. The religious–secular divide in Israel is a contemporary source of concern as relations between religious and secular are perceived as deteriorating to a potential "culture war" and a threat to Israel's social fabric. First, a struggle has taken place over what can be described as "liberal rights," against the Orthodox monopoly over issues of marriage, burial, and conversion. Second, the development of the market economy and a consumer culture have encouraged secular practices and undermined previous arrangements between religious and secular groups. This was matched by religious attempts to prevent the secularization of the public sphere.

The questions over the Orthodox monopoly became increasingly pertinent with globalization and the mass immigration from the FSU in the 1990s, which, respectively, accelerated the development of a market economy that defied religious norms and vastly increased the number of secular Jews unwilling to conform to religious norms and the number of non-Jews who could not be married in Israel. How will the state maintain its Jewish character? What will be the status of non-Jewish Israelis? What individual choice of marriage and other ceremonies will there be? Can religious norms regulate the free market of consumption? These are only a few of the questions that stem from this dilemma. Although alternative solutions and non-formal agreements have resolved some of these issues, the main questions over church and state and between Jewish and democratic are yet to be resolved.

What Does It Mean To Be an Israeli?

The two dilemmas above lead to a third one: what does it mean to be an Israeli? After more than fifty years of statehood an Israeli identity is still in flux, surveyed by immigration and religious and cultural differences. The definition of Israeliness embraces different issues, from national symbols to education curricula and citizenship rights. First and foremost, it is a question of the right of entry. Thus, immigration policies and realities confront Israelis with the challenges of definitions, whether with regard to immigrants whose Jewishness is questionable, foreign workers and refugees, or Palestinians claiming the right of return.

Beyond entry, the question of Israeliness is a question of culture in general and of specific rights and duties of citizenship. The cultural assimilation practiced in the early years of statehood is no longer performed, so immigrants, especially the large FSU immigration, can maintain their culture, and other groups can claim the same rights. This means that Israeli society will face the debate that other multicultural societies have faced: between individual rights, group rights, and the common good. To take a contemporary example, Ultra-Orthodox schools funded by the state have demanded that they be exempt from the teaching of English and mathematics required in other schools, to concentrate on Jewish studies. Against the group demand for autonomy arises the question of individual rights (pupils deprived of studying curricula that will allow them later on to choose their way of life, inside or outside the Orthodox community), but also a question of the common good: will these students be able later in life to integrate in the job market or will they remain poor and dependent on state allocations?

If being Israeli was previously a matter of contribution to the common good, both contribution and common good are now contested terms. The changes that the military has undergone described in chapter 5, is a case in point. Military service in the "people's army" was not only a legal obligation imbued with symbolic meaning; it was also constructed in terms of a community. But, military service, as a decisive standard by which rights were awarded to individuals and collectives, was also a source of hierarchy between Jews and non-Jews and men and women. The erosion of etatism, the political schism, and the evolvement of a consumer culture changed the status of the military as the old elites began to withdraw and peripheral groups came to replace them. What then will be considered a contribution, and to what common good, are likely to be debated in the coming years.

Social Rights, Economic Rights

In spite of its egalitarian-socialist image, gaps between center and periphery and between ethnic groups have always existed in Israel. In recent years, however, the growing gaps have seemed to shatter the myth of equality completely and to present another central dilemma of economic policy and economic rights. Israel's economic transformation since 1980 has turned it into, on the one hand, a Western-type globalized economy with a high-tech industry, a multinational labor force, and a thriving consumer culture but, on the other hand, a country with large gaps between rich and poor. Poverty in Israel overlaps with other divides – national, geographic, and ethnic – which make it an acute political problem.

Despite the dramatic economic changes, an open political debate involving citizens and political parties has not yet occurred, as economic policies seem to be beyond the public's reach, except in a few cases when specific groups in dire situations have taken their protest to the streets, with varying levels of success. The growth of third-sector organization and NGOs that ameliorate poverty are no substitute for engagement with the question of the state's obligations to its citizens and citizens' economic rights. Nevertheless, an economic debate is emerging through various civic society organizations with different social agendas. Whether Israel will rebuild its welfare state, take it apart, or create new institutions is another debate that lies ahead.

Who Will Make the Decisions?

The political stagnation and the loss of faith in the political parties are worrying signs for Israeli democracy and its capability to engage with the questions described above. Other institutions which were previously highly regarded, such as the Supreme Court and the military, are also losing some of their support, as the latter is seeing the withdrawal of the elites (see chapter 5) and the former the alienation of the religious right. The Supreme Court, however, remains a central arena of political struggle, as it is often preferred over the seemingly blocked political system but, paradoxically, its growing involvement makes it a political target in itself.

Another challenge comes from different sources of authority, especially religious ones. During the withdrawal from Gaza some Orthodox rabbis ordered their followers in the army to refuse to take part in the operation and to refuse army commands. Even a democratic decision of a majority, they explained, cannot justify the return of territories promised to the Jewish people by God. Consequently, it remains to be seen whether Israel has the democratic capacity not only to make decisions over its future borders but also to implement them.

The Road Ahead

Since 1980 Israel has accumulated significant challenges that are likely to remain with it in the near future, as it comes to terms with its new multicultural realities and attempts to determine its internal and external boundaries. The schisms described above and throughout the book overload the political system and erode political trust in institutions and between groups. These tensions, on the one hand, make it difficult to make decisions on the crucial dilemmas that lie ahead, but, on the other hand, require that genuine efforts be made.

Conflict is not the inevitable outcome of existing ethnic, religious, or cultural differences. Rather, the consolidation and politicization of these differences can take different paths that depend, at least to some extent, on political choices being made. The question, in other words, is not only what different groups want, but also what opportunities are offered by the state and what effects its official ideologies, institutions, and policies have on identity and mobilization: it is about creating the right institutions that would provide the right answers.

Like other democratic states, Israel since 1980 has reached a crossroads at which decisions must be made and postponements are no longer possible. Israelis – Arabs and Jews, religious and secular, veteran and immigrants – have shown great resourcefulness and have taken their fate in their own hands rather than succumb to the stagnant political system. These actions have not always been positive (and often less than that), but show a dynamic society capable of change. It remains to be seen whether this dynamism will erode Israeli society, heighten segregation, and undermine democracy or, alternatively, will bring new ideas and incentives that cross current divisions, and, from the existing grass-root level, will energize the stagnant political system.

Index

Page numbers in bold refer to tables; those in italics refer to figures